MW01031414

Caring Kitchens Recipes

by
Gloria Lawson

TEACH Services, Inc.
Brushton, New York

Printing History

1989 1st Edition
1992 2nd Edition
1993 3rd Edition

Printed in the United States of America

ISBN 0-945383-63-0

Library of Congress number: 93-61485

Consumer and Corporate Affairs Canada
Reg. No. 387936

Published by

TEACH Services, Inc.
Donivan Road
Route 1, Box 182
Brushton, New York 12916

Specializing in recipes for better health featuring:

Natural whole grains,

Tasty vegetarian,

Dairy–free,

Nourishing desserts,

Healthful recipes.

"Cooking…is a science…its right use has much to do with keeping…health.
It is the most valuable of all gifts…food should be prepared with care…"

Counsels on Diet and Foods, pg. 251, 259.

"Be kind to the animals ... don't eat them!"

Dedicated

To all who have given
generously of their time
and love in our Cooking
Schools throughout the years.

"God desires only the service of love."
Desire of Ages, p. 22.

Illustrator	*Denis LeBlanc*
Design	*Kris LeBlanc*
Needlework for covers	*Stephanie Preston Diemert*
Back cover photo	*Bob LaChance*
Photography	*Russ Salamon*

ACKNOWLEDGEMENTS

It must make Jesus happy to see unselfishness, "a love that seeketh not her own." This love has been witnessed in putting this little book together. A special thank you to Denis LeBlanc, who did all the beautiful art work, and to his wife Kris. As Denis humbly said, "It was God who guided my hand, give Him the glory." Thank you Denis, for every work of art, every gift of love.

When it came time to type the recipes, God again worked a miracle by providing an Apple Mac computer. By a series of providences, we met Randy Wilson, a complete stranger, who lives two or three miles from us–who offered to loan us his personal computer, software, printer, and everything. Weekend after weekend Randy would bring his computer over and set it up in our living room. He too, freely gave, accepting no remuneration. A special thank you, Randy, for your generosity.

Thank you, Paul, my husband, for your support, proofing, sampling, suggestions, washing dishes, and encouragement.

A special thank you to my mother–Mable Nash, Ursula Krahne, Carole Minnick, Lorraine Barker, Donna Hastings, Gizella Lawson, Ellen and Shirley Laan, Josie Jarnevic, Mary Lutyk, Bonnie Laing and Helen Cate. Thank you, Joan Barker, for your help with recipes. Thank you Vicki Skinder, for designing the "All Fruit" Fruit Cake, and Bob LaChance for taking the picture shown on the back cover of this book. Not to be forgotten are those who helped in other ways, expecially; Kris LeBlanc, Barbara Kozarichuk, Jean Strifling, Marla King, and Bonnie Wallace. A special thank you to each of you.

"Every act of love,
every word of kindness,
is reported before the eternal throne
and placed on heaven's imperishable
record."

My Life Today, p. 237.

Read the recipes carefully,
Follow directions exactly,
Garnish creations artistically,
Serve your family lovingly.

Please note:

- **Cooking temperatures** given are all in degrees Fahrenheit (i.e., 350° F.).
- The **"Mock Chicken" Seasonings** used in these recipes are special recipes shared in the "Seasoning Section". They have no additives, MSG, or harmful spices that are gastric irritants.
- **If using sea salt** to make onion salt or garlic salt, use equal amounts of sea salt and powders.
- **"Home Spray"** to grease all pans, casserole dishes, etc. In spray bottle—add:

  1 c. corn oil
  1 T. liquid soy lecithin

  Mix well by shaking.
  Spray lightly and brush on—nothing sticks!
- Wherever a recipe calls for you to sauté an ingredient, I would highly recommend (as a progressive measure), to gradually cut down the oil to as little as 1 teaspoon of oil to 1-2 tablespoon of water, and eventually just in water.
- Arrowroot powder and every ingredient has been chosen with care.
- **Please read the glossary for successful tips.**

Best wishes in your venture in healthful, vegetarian cooking!

With Love,
Gloria

Table of Contents

The Five Food Groups

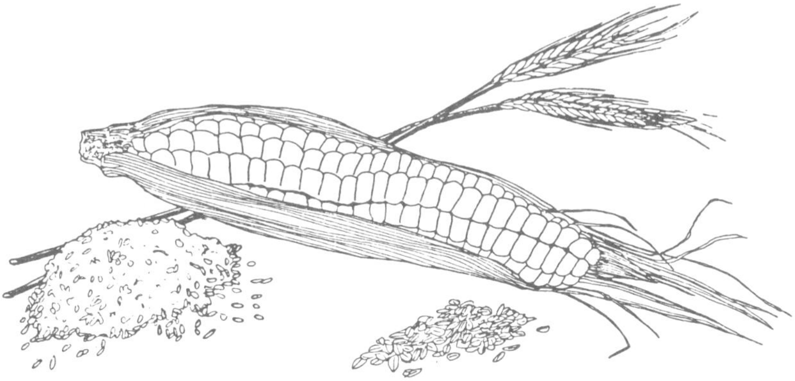

Grains

Vegetables

Nuts and Seeds

Legumes

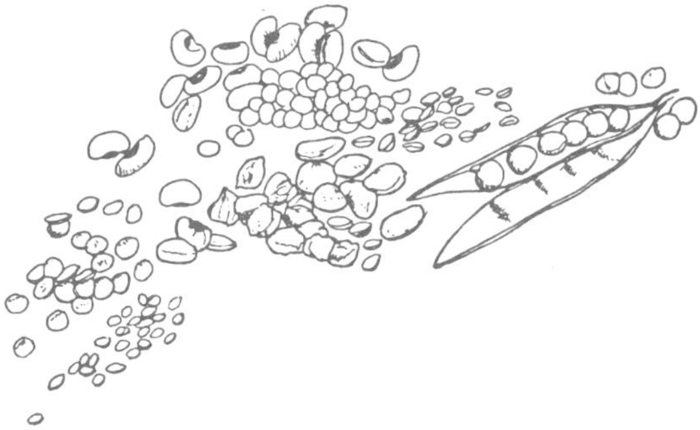

Fruit

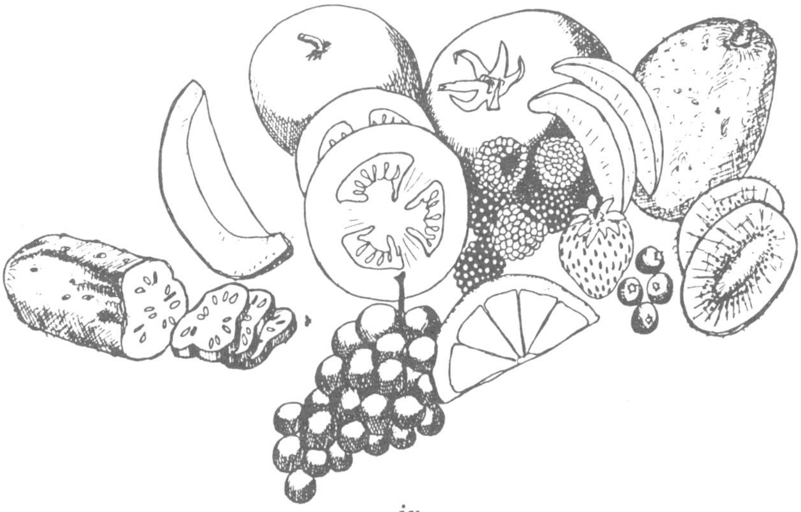

Notes

GLOSSARY

Abbreviations And Definitions Of Foods

T. Tablespoon
t. teaspoon
c. cup
p. page

Agar agar flakes A vegetable gelatin made from sea weeds into flakes. 1T. agar agar flakes = 1 t. agar agar powder.

Arrowroot powder A starch obtained from several tropical, American plants, by grinding the root into a powder. It is used as a thickener (like cornstarch) and the result is a smooth texture. It can be used to thicken spreads, puddings, gravies, sauces, soups, etc.

Bisto A gravy mix with a savory flavor. The ingredients are cornstarch, salt, wheat starch, caramel, defatted soyaflour, hydrolyzed plant protein, Torula yeast, carrot powder and onion powder (1 T. Bisto = 1 t. beef-style seasoning).

Blanch Place fruit or almonds in boiling water for a short period of time, in order to remove the skins easily. Almonds should be skinned immediately after blanching or scalding—don't leave in boiling water but a few seconds.

Bran The coarse, outer coat of grains or fibre. It may be added to cereals to give more roughage in the diet as desired.

Bulgar Wheat is a partially cooked, cracked whole wheat product which is used in Tebula Salad and some patties. Bring 2 cups of water to boil, add 1/4 t. salt, 1 c. Bulgar wheat and simmer 10–15 minutes until reconstituted. It is delicious as a cereal with dates.

Carob Powder Commonly called "St. John's Bread". Carob is a chocolate substitute and should be purchased without sugar and added to suggested treats. 1 T. carob powder has 28 mg. calcium in it, and 6 mg. phosphorus. It is much lower in fat than chocolate—2% instead of 52% and does not contain caffeine or stimulating substances. Should be available at health food stores. Use dark carob in all recipes.

Cashews used in all recipes are raw and should be washed in hot water before using.

Coconut The unsweetened shredded coconut (desiccated) is used in these recipes.

Mock Chicken Seasoning #1 (see p. 119) and #2 (see p. 119). No harmful spices or additives are used. (1 T. Mock Chicken Seasoning #2 = 1-1/4 t. commercial chicken-style seasoning)

Cous Cous is made from coarsely ground durum wheat—which has been pre-cooked. It is a traditional dish of North Africa and Morocco.

Dextrinized Uncooked whole grains such as rice, wheat kernels (berries), rye, oats, cornmeal, cracked wheat, etc., are dextrinized by heating the grain in a heavy cast iron skillet (or an electric frying pan set at 300°) until very light brown, stirring constantly to prevent burning. This procedure shortens the cooking time by almost half and improves the flavor. The whole grain kernels will not necessarily turn brown but will make a popping noise. Dextrinized grains are easier to digest. The complex starches are broken down to simpler starches and sugars.

Engevita Yeast is a very nutritious powder—high in protein, vitamins and minerals, and has a delightful flavor. Nutritional yeast flakes may be substituted for Engevita Yeast in recipes. It adds a "cheesy" flavor to Cashew Pimento Cheese and can be added to patties for nutrition and flavor. It is the base for the Mock Chicken Seasoning and many recipes.

Flours and grains referred to in these recipes are whole grain unless otherwise indicated. If using any white flour—use unbleached white flour.

Grease Pans with "Home Spray" so food will not stick.

"Home Spray"—Mix together well:

1 c.	**corn oil**
1 T.	**liquid soy lecithin**

Put in spray bottle and brush on pans.

Legumes Beans, peas, peanuts or lentils, etc.

Lemon Juice Use in place of vinegar. Vinegar is a gastric irritant.

Maggi "Aroma" used in place of soy sauce. Ingredients are hydrolyzed vegetable protein, water and salt. Knorr liquid or Bragg Liquid Aminos may be used instead of Maggi if preferred (same ingredients).

Oat Flakes Large flakes.

Quick Oats Smaller flakes and quick cooking. Anything with oats should stand at least 5 minutes to absorb liquids before making patties or shaping cookies.

Pastry flour is made from soft wheat. If using stone-ground whole wheat pastry flour and the recipe calls for 1 c.—use 1/4 c. less. Recipes will note whether to use stone-ground pastry flour or not. If not available, use 2 c. whole wheat pastry flour instead of 1-1/2 c. stone-ground whole wheat pastry flour in whole wheat pastry recipe. Do not adjust recipes—just follow directions.

Sesame Seeds Unhulled, are used in these recipes. They are very high in calcium and most nutritious.

Soymilk may be made from recipe in cookbook—or use "Loma Linda Soyagen" which contains no cane or beet sugar. Nutmilks may be substituted for soymilk.

Sprouts Grown from seeds, in your kitchen for added nutrition—something fresh!

Tahini A seed butter, like peanut butter, made from hulled sesame seeds. Sesame butter is made from the unhulled sesame seeds, and has a stronger flavor.

Tofu is also known as "soybean curd". It is made from soymilk much like cottage cheese and pressed into blocks. Firm tofu is used in these recipes. When opened, place in container and cover with cold water. The water should be changed daily until the tofu is used. Tofu is high in protein, and acts as a binder in recipes. It is very versatile because of its bland flavor and smooth texture. It can be scrambled like eggs, made into soy cottage cheese with seasonings, or added to fruit and used as a soy yogurt.

Utensils Use "Silverstone" for non-sticking cookie sheets, muffin tins and for baking. Especially cooking and baking with natural foods—as dates in cookies—they burn less and you get top quality results. Some patties will stick if not using a "Silverstone" frying pan. The real benefits are, less or no oil, and they don't stick. "Pyrex" or "Corning Wear" dishes—for casseroles, roasts and loaves.

COOKING WITH NATURAL FOODS

"Health is a treasure. Of all temporal possessions it is the most precious." *Counsels on Diet and Foods*, p. 20. Health is not by chance—but choice.

"Jesus saith unto him, I am the way, the truth, and the life:..." John 14:6.

"Grains, fruits, nuts and vegetables constitute the diet chosen for us by our Creator. These foods prepared in as simple and natural a manner as possible, are the most healthful and nourishing. They impart a strength, a power of endurance, a vigor of intellect, that are not afforded by a more complex and stimulating diet." *Ibid.*, p. 81. The Creator's original diet is still the best—Genesis 1:29.

GUIDELINES FOR A PROPER DIET

1. "Be temperate in eating." *Ibid.*, pg. 82., "serve with simplicity and...nicety." *Ibid.*, pg. 110.
2. Avoid rich and luxurious foods—spices and fats.
3. Regularity in meals.
4. Eating nothing between meals.
5. "Use simple, wholesome food." *Ibid.*, pg. 87.
6. "...diet should be suited to the season, ...climate...and...the occupation..." *Ibid.*, pg. 94.
7. Eat a variety of foods—from day to day—but not a big variety at one meal—e.g. 3 or 4 dishes per meal. Too many varieties cause fermentation in the stomach.
8. The ideal is "...to have the fruit at one meal, and the vegetables at another." *Ibid.*, pg. 112.

"If we would preserve the best health, we should avoid eating vegetables and fruit at the same meal. If the stomach is feeble, there will be distress, the brain will be confused, and unable to put forth mental effort. Have fruit at one meal and vegetables at the next..." *Counsels on Diet and Foods*, page 395.

"It is not well to eat fruit and vegetables at the same meal." *Ibid.*, pg 112.

What is a fruit and what is a vegetable?

- **The fruit** has a seed or seeds in it, such as peaches, nectarines, plums, oranges, grapefruit, pears, grapes and bananas, etc. There are black berries, raspberries, strawberries, blueberries, also cucumbers, squash, tomatoes, green peppers, eggplant and green beans.
- **Vegetables** are the leaf, stem, root or flower of the plant such as spinach, kale, celery, rhubarb, potatoes, carrots, beets, and broccoli.
- **Seeds:** All grains—rye, wheat, oats, rice, etc. Nuts—almonds, filberts, pecans, walnuts Legumes—kidney beans, pinto beans, lentils, garbanzos, peanuts, etc. Seeds—pumpkin, sunflower, sesame

<u>The seeds can be eaten with fruit or vegetables.</u>

9. "The various preparations of rice, wheat, corn, and oats are sent abroad everywhere, also beans, peas, and lentils. These, with native or imported fruits, and the variety of vegetables that grow in each locality, give an opportunity to select a dietary that is complete without the use of flesh meats.... Wherever dried fruits, such as raisins, prunes, apples, pears, peaches, and apricots, are obtainable at moderate prices, it will be found that they can be used as staple articles of diet much more freely...." *Counsels on Diet and Foods,* pg. 94, 95.

10. **Eat fruit**—freely.

    "The more we depend upon the fresh fruit just as it is plucked from the tree, the greater will be the blessing." Ibid., p. 96.

PROBLEMS TO AVOID:

1. Overeating
   - makes one sluggish
   - may cause bad breath
   - more tired
   - forgetful
   - causes irritability
2. Avoid study or vigorous exercise right after eating.
3. Digestion hindered by too much liquid in the diet.
4. Eating in a hurry.
5. Milk and sugar combined are liable to cause fermentation in the stomach.
6. Avoid eating late at night.

BENEFITS OF A VEGETARIAN AND NATURAL FOODS DIET

1. Better health and promotes longer life.
2. Helps prevent degenerative diseases.
3. High in fiber.
4. Rich in vitamins and minerals.
5. More economical.
6. Increased strength and endurance.
7. Lower in calories—an aid to weight control.
8. Original—goes back to the source.
9. Lowers incidence of all forms of cancer and heart diseases.

Doctor Astrand, *Director of Physiology Institute* in Stockholm, Sweden, conducted a study on trained athletes measuring their level of endurance on different diets. The athletes were placed on ergometers (exercise bicycles) and their endurance tested at 70% of their work load capacity, measured by the length of time they could keep up a set speed against a measured resistance.

		Continuous Exercise Till Exhaustion
Phase One	Normal diet such as meat, potatoes, carrots, margarine, cabbage and milk.	1 hr., 54 min.
Phase Two	High protein and fat diet from animal products such as meats, fish, butter and eggs.	57 min.
Phase Three	High carbohydrate diet, such as bread, potatoes, corn and various vegetables and fruits.	2 hr., 47 min.

From "Taste of Nature Cooking School" class participation Magazine No. 1. Used by permission of Gary Strunk.

Baking Powder and Baking Soda

Baking powders and soda destroy some thiamine and irritate the lining of the digestive tract.

"The one who understands the art of properly preparing food, and who uses this knowledge, is worthy of higher commendation than those engaged in any other line of work. This talent should be regarded as equal in value to TEN talents; for its right use has much to do with keeping the human organism in health. Because so inseparably connected with life and health, it is the most valuable of all gifts." *Counsels on Diet and Foods,* p. 251.

SUGGESTED DAILY PROGRAM

"In grains, fruits, vegetables and nuts are to be found all the food elements that we need." *Counsels on Diet and Foods,* p. 92.

Upon rising—1 or 2 glasses of water.

Vary the menus—for nutritious meals.

Suggested Menus—for 1 day

A GENEROUS BREAKFAST

2 fruits—1 raw—and high in Vitamin "C"
Whole grain cereal
Whole grain bread
Spread—nut spread, avocado, or
  dried fruit marmalade (see p. 175)
Nut milk or Soy milk
  (If not using nut milks or nut spreads—include 1 protein food, e.g. 2 T. sunflower seeds—or nuts, etc.)

ALLOW 5–6 HOURS BETWEEN MEALS

MIDMORNING—1 glass of water and 1 more—1/2 hr. before dinner

NOON MEAL—Main meal if possible

Main protein dish
Potato or rice
1 green or yellow vegetable rich in Vitamin "A"
Raw salad
Bread and spread
Simple dessert—optional

MID-AFTERNOON—1 glass of water and 1 more—1/2 hr. before supper

SUPPER—lightest meal of the day
Soup—or fruit salad—or fruit
Sandwich—with whole grain bread—or toast or whole grain crackers or breadsticks

EVENING—1 glass water

MEAL PLANNING SUGGESTIONS

1. Plan meals—for several days in advance. Decide on an entrée and select other foods to complement and complete the meal.
2. Plan different breakfasts—e.g. wholegrain waffles, nut french toast (see p. 127), fruit toast (see p. 143), etc.
3. Choose a variety of wholesome foods from day to day, prepared as simply and attractively as possible.
4. Use in as natural a manner as possible.
5. Provide contrast in flavor, color and texture in meals.
6. Have meals at regular times to avoid snacking or nibbling.
7. Chew your food well. Eat in a relaxed and cheerful attitude.
8. Avoid rich desserts, highly spiced and fatty meats.

Happy Eating!

"Persons who have accustomed themselves to a rich, highly stimulating diet, have an unnatural taste, and they cannot at once relish food that is plain and simple. It will take time for the taste to become natural, and for the stomach to recover from the abuse it has suffered. But those who persevere in the use of wholesome food will, after a time, find it palatable. Its delicate and delicious flavors will be appreciated, and it will be eaten with greater enjoyment than can be derived from unwholesome dainties." *Counsels on Diet and Foods,* pg.84.

Proteins

"Nuts and nut foods are coming largely into use to take the place of flesh meats. With nuts may be combined grains, fruits, and some roots, to make foods that are healthful and nourishing. Care should be taken, however, not to use too large a proportion of nuts. Those who realize ill effects from the use of nut foods may find the difficulty removed by attending to this precaution." *Ibid.*, p. 363, 364.

"The animals are diseased, and by partaking of their flesh, we plant the seeds of disease in our own tissue and blood." *Ibid.* p. 386.

"A meat diet changes the disposition and strengthens animalism." *Ibid.*, p. 386.

Total Vegetarians: combine plant proteins.

"Grains such as wheat, corn, and polished rice, (which are high in the amino acid methionine and low in the amino acid lysine) can be combined with legumes such as lentils, beans, peas or certain nuts (which are just the opposite—high in lysine and low in methionine). These foods do not need to be eaten together at the same meal.... Something from both groups during the day seems to work just as well." Comments by Kenneth I. Burke, Ph.D. and Ann C. Burke. *Vibrant Life*, Jan/Feb. '85.

Vegetable Protein Combinations:

Wheat	with	Legumes: e.g. black-eyed peas, garbanzos (chick peas), kidney beans, lima beans, navy beans, peanuts, pinto beans and soy beans
Rice	with	Legumes, Sesame seeds, Wheat
Legumes	with	Barley, Corn, Oats, Rice, Sesame Seeds, Wheat

Sample Amino Acid Comparisons
(100 mg. *or* 3-1/2 oz.)

	Tryptophan	Leucine	Lysine	Methionine
Whole Wheat	160	891	359	200
Kidney Beans	202	1935	1665	225
Beef	219	1509	1387	403
Sesame Seeds	309	1583	546	601
Sunflower Seeds	360	1824	912	456
2 Med. Eggs	198	1092	794	284

Taste of "Nature Cooking School" class participation Magazine No.1. Used by permission of Gary Strunk.

Entrées

LASAGNA

Place by layers in a 13" x 9" x 2" Pyrex dish:

2-1/2 c. Parmigiana Sauce (see p. 12)
Lasagna strips, uncooked or precooked*
3 c. Tofu Cottage Cheese (see p. 12) use plain tofu
2/3 c. Cashew Pimento Cheese Sauce (see p. 65)

Repeat above layers, using 3/4 c. Cashew Pimento Cheese Sauce instead of 2/3 c. on last layer. Bake at 350° F. for 1 hour. This dish is best made ahead of time and reheated as the mixture sets up better when cooled and reheated.

*or thinly slice zucchini lengthwise and use in place of pasta.

PARMIGIANA SAUCE

Place in a large saucepan:

8 c. tomatoes, canned
2–3 T. honey or to taste
1/4 t. oregano
2 t. sweet basil
2 T. onion powder
1/4 t. garlic powder
salt to taste
2 t. arrowroot powder dissolved in 1 T. water

Bring to a boil. Cook until thick.
Note: If using as a gravy for patties, add more thickening.

TOFU COTTAGE CHEESE FOR LASAGNA

In colander, squeeze excess liquid from:

6 c. tofu (about 6 cubes)

Add and mash all together:

3/4 t. salt
1-1/2 t. onion powder
1/2 t. garlic powder
1/3 c. Soy Mayonnaise (see p. 83)

Refrigerate.

EGGPLANT PARMIGIANA

Cut an eggplant in 1/2" slices lengthwise. Dip slices in soy or nut milk, then in fine Seasoned Bread Crumbs (see p. 13). Place slices on cookie sheet. Bake on each side until nearly tender in 350° F. oven.

Spread Parmigiana Sauce (see p. 12) on eggplant 1/2" from edge. Spread Tofu Cottage Cheese (see p. 78) on top of sauce. Top with Pimento Cheese Spread (see p. 167).

Bake at 350° F. for 35 minutes.

SEASONED BREAD CRUMBS

Mix well:

1/2 c. flour, unbleached white
1/2 t. onion salt
1/4 t. garlic powder
1/4 c. bread crumbs, whole wheat, toasted, very fine
1/4 t. salt or to taste
1 T. Engevita yeast (see p. 2)

CHEEZY MEATBALLS

In large bowl:

2 c. tofu, firm, crumbled fine (about 2 cubes)
1 c. Cashew Pimento Cheese Sauce (see p. 65)
4 t. onion powder
1/2 t. sage
2 t. dried parsley, powdered
1/4 t. garlic powder
1 c. bread crumbs, fresh
3/4 c. pecans, ground *or* **chopped fine**
1/2 t. salt or to taste

Mix well. Form into mini patties or meatballs and fry in a Silverstone frying pan with a trickle of oil.

For vegetable meal add:

1 sm. *or* **med. onion, chopped fine**
2 T. parsley, fresh snipped with scissors for small pieces

Adjust salt to taste.

ALMOND RICE PATTIES

Sauté lightly in 1 t. oil and 1 T. water:

1 med.-lg. onion, chopped fine
2/3 c. celery, chopped fine (about 2 stalks)
1/4 t. salt

Put above ingredients in a bowl.

Add:
3/4 c. tofu, crumbled
2 c. brown rice, cooked
1 T. Engevita yeast (see p. 2)
1/4 t. sage
1 t. Maggi (see p. 2)
1/2 t. onion salt
1/4 t. garlic powder
1/4 t. celery salt
1/2 c. oats, quick

Blend in blender till creamy:
1/2 c. almonds, blanched
1/2 c. water

Combine all and mix well. Drop by spoonfuls and fry on Silverstone frying pan with a trickle of oil until golden on each side.

CASHEW LOAF

In large bowl:

3/4 c. cashews, raw, coarsely ground
1 c. soymilk
1 med. onion, chopped very fine
1 c. bread crumbs, whole wheat bread, fresh
1 T. Maggi (see p. 2)
1/4 t. salt
2 T. dried parsley, powdered with fingers
or **1/4 c. parsley, fresh snipped with scissors**
1/4 t. celery seed
1/4 c. oats, quick

Mix well. Pour in greased baking dish. Bake at 350° F. for 45 minutes or until firm and lightly golden.

CHRISTMAS PATTIES

In bowl: **2-1/2 c. rice, cooked** (1-1/4 c. cooked Lundberg brown rice *and* 1-1/4 c. cooked basmati white rice)

Blend in blender until creamy and add to above:

1/3 c. almonds, blanched
1/3 c. water

Add: **2/3 c. cashews, coarsley ground**
2 T. + 1 t. Mock Chicken Seasoning #2 (see p. 119)
1/2 t. garlic salt
3/4 t. onion salt
1/2 c. soymilk
1 c. tofu, crumbled (about 1 cube)
1/4 t. celery salt
1/2 c. oats, quick

Mix well, shape into patties—and fry in a trickle of oil on a Silverstone frying pan until golden on each side.

PECAN PATTIES

Mix in large bowl:

2-1/4 c. tofu, crumbled
2/3 c. pecans, ground
1/3 c. walnuts, ground
2 c. water
3 t. Maggi (see p. 2)
3 T. Bisto (see p. 1)
1/2 t. garlic salt
1 t. onion powder
1/4 t. celery salt
1 c. bread crumbs, whole wheat, fresh, firmly packed
2 c. oats, quick
1/4 t. sage

Form into patties and fry on Silverstone frying pan with a trickle of oil. Brown on medium-low heat about 5 minutes on each side.

Suggestion: serve with Parmigiana Sauce (see p. 12) with sautéed green pepper.

TOFU PECAN LOAF

Mix in large bowl:

- **1 c. pecans, ground**
- **1-1/4 c. tofu, crumbled and mashed**
- **2/3 c. soymilk**
- **1 c. brown rice, cooked**
- **1 c. celery, chopped very fine**
- **1 med. onion, chopped fine**
- **1/4 t. celery salt**
- **1/2 t. onion salt**
- **1/2 t. garlic salt**
- **1 T. Maggi (see p. 2)**

Mix well and put in greased Pyrex loaf dish.
Cover and bake at 350° F.—45 minutes.
Uncover—bake at 350° F.—15 minutes or until set and golden.

For Fruit Meal add 1/2 c. green pepper, chopped fine, instead of celery and onion.

NUTTY NUT PATTIES

To reconstitute bulgar wheat, place in a small pot:

- **1-1/3 c. water, boiling**
- **2/3 c. bulgar wheat (see p. 1)**
- **1/4 t. salt**

Bring to boil and simmer on lowest heat for 15 minutes. Remove from heat and let cool.
Add above to large bowl.

Add:
- **1/2 c. pecans *or* walnuts, chopped fine**
- **3/4 c. oats, quick**
- **3 T. Bisto (see p. 1)**
- **1 t. onion powder**
- **1/4 t. sage**
- **1/2 t. garlic salt or to taste**
- **1/2 c. soy *or* nut milk**
- **1 c. tofu, well drained** (about 1 cube)
- **1 t. Maggi (see p. 2)**

continued...

Mix well and form into patties. Drop onto Silverstone frying pan rubbed lightly with oil. Brown on medium-low heat.

Optional: Use 2 cups cooked brown rice in place of bulgar wheat.

WALNUT TOFU PUFFS

Sauté lightly in 1 T. olive oil:

1 med.-lg. **onion, chopped fine**
1 lg. clove **garlic, chopped fine**
1/8 t. **salt**

Add the above ingredients and combine in large bowl:

2 c. **tofu, well drained and crumbled** (about 2 cubes)
2 T. **Bisto** **(see p. 1)**
1 T. **Maggi** **(see p. 2)**
2/3 c. **walnuts, ground**
1 T. **dried parsley flakes**
or **2 T. parsley, fresh chopped, fine**
1/4 t. **celery salt**
1/4 t. **sage**
1/4 t. **garlic salt**
3/4 c. **brown rice, cooked**
1-1/2 c. **bread crumbs, whole wheat, fresh**

Mix well and shape into meat balls.
Fry until golden in Silverstone frying pan with a trickle of oil. Turn frequently so all sides are browned.

TOFU ORIENTAL

Sauté in 1 T. oil:

1 lg. **onion, cut in big pieces**
1/4 t. **salt**

Add:2–3 c.of 1" cubes of tofu

Season according to taste with:

Bisto **(see p. 1)**
Maggi **(see p. 2)**
Salt

Serve on fluffy brown rice.

To Freeze Tofu Slices (for following recipes):
Drain tofu and cut in 1/4" thick slices.
Freeze individually on cookie sheet.
Place in container with wax paper between frozen slices. Freeze until ready to use.

TOFU STEAKS

Thaw desired amount of tofu slices. (If in a hurry, pour boiling water over frozen tofu, then drain and press water out.)

Sprinkle Maggi (see p. 2) lightly on each side.
Pat tofu steak generously in following seasonings:

1/2 c. flour, white unbleached
2 T. Bisto (see p. 1)
1/4 t. garlic salt

Fry until crunchy-crisp in a trickle of oil in Silverstone frying pan.

Optional: Add onions while frying.

TOFU CHICK

Sprinkle Maggi (see p. 2) lightly on each side.
Pat thawed tofu slices generously in following seasonings. Mix well in bowl:

1/2 c. flour, unbleached white
1/2 t. celery salt
4 t. Mock Chicken Seasoning #2 (see p. 119)
1/2 t. onion salt
1 T. Engevita yeast (see p. 2)

Fry until crunchy-crisp in a trickle of oil in Silverstone frying pan. Serve with fresh lemon wedges.

There are but few who realize that in order to enjoy health and cheerfulness, they must have an abundance of sunlight, pure air, and physical exercise. My Life Today, p. 138.

HERBED SAVORETTES

In large bowl:

1-1/4 c. tofu, crumbled
2/3 c. walnuts, ground coarse
1/2 t. salt
1/2 c. soymilk
1/2 c. oats, quick
1/4 t. basil
1/4 t. thyme
1/4 t. sage
1 t. Maggi (see p. 2)
1 stalk celery, chopped very fine
1 sm. onion, chopped very fine
1/4 c. parsley, chopped very fine
2 t. Mock Chicken Seasoning #2 (see p. 119)
1 c. bread crumbs, whole wheat, fresh

Mix well. Form into patties and fry on medium low heat in Silverstone frying pan with a trickle of oil until golden on each side.

ELAINE'S NUT LOAF

Sauté in 1 T. oil:

1 med. onion, chopped fine

Add sautéed onions to large bowl.

Add: 1-1/2 c. brown rice, cooked
1/2 c. oat flakes, large (regular)
1/2 c. walnuts, ground fine
3/4 t. salt
3/4 c. soymilk
2 t. Maggi (see p. 2)
2 T. Mock Chicken Seasoning #1 (see p. 119)
1 c. tofu, crumbled

Mix well. Pour into greased 8" x 8" Pyrex dish.
Bake at 350° F. for 1 hour.

BROCCOLI SUPREME

Bake Elaine's Nut Loaf (see p. 19) in an 8" x 8" or equivalent size Pyrex dish.

Wash and cut broccoli flowerettes in individual flowers with a little stem.

Steam broccoli 5 minutes or until still crunchy.
Drain well.
On top of Elaine's Nut Loaf (heated) attractively place broccoli flowerettes.

Trickle Cashew Pimento Cheese (see p. 65) over broccoli stems, or as desired. Reheat in oven at 350° F. until "cheese" is heated.

BON MILLET PATTI

Blend in blender until creamy (1 minute):

1/4 c. almonds
1/4 c. water

Add and blend: **1/2 c. water**

Mix the above in a large bowl with:

1 c. tofu (about 1 cube)
3/4 c. oats, quick
1/4 c. cashews, ground fine
1/2 t. garlic salt
2 T. Mock Chicken Seasoning #2 (see p. 119)
1/2 t. salt
2-1/2 c. millet, cooked and salted
1/4 t. sweet basil
1 t. Maggi (see p. 2)
1 med. onion, chopped fine and sautéed in water until tender
or **1 t. onion powder**

Drop by rounded tablespoonsful onto Silverstone frying pan rubbed lightly with oil. Brown on medium-low heat 7 minutes each side.

CREAMY MILLET LOAF

Blend in blender until creamy:

2/3 c. almonds, freshly blanched
2/3 c. water

When thick add 1/2 c. additional water and continue blending.

Add: **1/4 t. celery salt**
1/2 t. garlic salt
1 t. onion salt
2 T. Engevita yeast (see p. 2)

Pour above mixture in a large bowl.

Add: **1 c. millet seed, hulled**
3 c. tomato juice
1 c. water
2/3 c. black olives, sliced or chopped (optional)
2 T. Mock Chicken Seasoning #2 (see p. 119)

Mix well and pour into large greased casserole or large flat Pyrex dish, about 2" deep.

Cover. Bake at 350° F. for 1 hour.
Remove lid or foil wrap and bake additional 15 minutes. Turn off oven and let sit 15 minutes (firms up as it sits).

Note: Baking time will depend on depth of pan (shallow pan—less time).

Pure water is one of Heaven's choicest blessings.
The Ministry of Healing, p. 237.

Regularity in eating is very important for health of body and serenity of mind. Counsels on Health, p. 118.

CARROT RICE LOAF

Sauté in 1 T. oil and 3 T. water:

1 med.-lg. onion, chopped fine

Add to the above in large bowl:

2 c. carrots, grated fine
2 c. brown rice, cooked
1/2 t. garlic powder
1/2 c. walnuts, ground
1-1/2 c. soymilk *or* **nutmilk**
1/4 t. sage
3/4 t. salt or to taste
1 t. onion powder
3 slices bread, whole wheat, fresh, made into crumbs

Mix well. Put in greased Pyrex dish. Sprinkle paprika on top before baking. Bake at 350° F. for 45 minutes or until loaf is set.

EGGPLANT PATTIES—*a favorite!*

1 lg. eggplant, washed, (leave skin on and cut in small crouton size cubes; about = 7-1/2—8 cups)

Add: **3/4 c. water**

Bring to boil then lower heat and simmer 5 minutes.
Drain and mash eggplant.
In large bowl, add to the above mixture:

2/3 c. walnuts, ground
1 c. bread crumbs
3/4 c. oats, quick
1/2 t. garlic salt
1/4 t. celery salt
1/2 t. onion salt
1/4 t. sage
1 t. Maggi (see p. 2)

Mix well. Let stand 5 minutes. Fry in lightly oiled Silverstone frying pan on medium heat—5 minutes on each side.

Note: If lesser amount of eggplant is used—adjust salts.

CELERY SOUFFLÉ

Sauté in frying pan with 1 T. oil

1 med.-lg. onion, chopped fine
1-1/2 c. celery, chopped fine
1 clove garlic, minced

Simmer lightly. Remove from heat.
Add to the above, in a large bowl:

1/3 c. parsley, fresh snipped with scissors for small pieces
3 "Shredded Wheat" (cereal) thoroughly crumbled
1 c. tofu, crumbled (about 1 cube)

Blend in blender for 1 minute

1/2 c. almonds, blanched
1/2 c. and 2 T. water
1/4 t. salt
3 T. Mock Chicken Seasoning #2 (see p. 119)

Add: **1 c. water**
1 t. Maggi (see p. 2)
1/2 t. celery salt
1/2 t. onion salt
1/4 t. garlic salt

Add the blender mixture to the bowl mixture.
Rinse out blender with 1/4 c. water and add to bowl mixture.
Mix lightly.
Pour in greased loaf pan. Sprinkle paprika on top.
Bake at 350° F. for 50 minutes.
Remove lid and bake an additional 10 minutes.

Health is a great treasure. It is the richest possession that mortals can have. Counsels to Teachers, p. 286.

GREEN RICE CASSEROLE

In a small Silverstone frying pan:

1/4 c. water
1-1/2 c. celery, chopped fine
1 med.- lg. onion, chopped fine
1/4 t. salt

Steam until lightly done. Place in large casserole.

Add: **3 c. brown rice (Lundberg), cooked**

Blend in blender until creamy—1 minute:

1/2 c. almonds, blanched
1/2 c. + 2 T. water

Add: **1/4 c. water**
2 T. Mock Chicken Seasoning #2 (see p. 119)

Pour over rice in casserole.

Add: **1/4 t. garlic salt**
1/2 t. onion salt
1/4 c. parsley, fresh snipped with scissors in small pieces

Mix well. Sprinkle a little paprika on top.
Cover and bake at 350° F. for 45 minutes. Uncover and bake for an additional 10 minutes.

Note: If in a flat casserole, bake less time as it just has to heat through, and remove the lid to brown a little on top.

SPINACH QUICHE

(a daughter-in-law's favorite)

Bake a 10" x 2" deep pie shell at 425° F. for 7 minutes.

Blend until creamy (1 minute):

1 c. cashews, raw
1 c. water

Add and blend:

2 T. Mock Chicken Seasoning #1 (see p. 119)
1/4 t. garlic salt
1/2 t. salt
2 T. arrowroot powder

continued...

1/2 t. onion powder
2 c. tofu, well drained

Cook in boiling water until tender:

2–10 oz. pkgs. spinach, fresh (drained well, chopped = 1-1/2 cups)
1/2 t. salt

Put blended mixture in bowl. Fold in spinach. Pour mixture into partially baked shell. Bake at 350° F. for 40 minutes.

FAVORITE SPINACH PATTIES

Cook until tender:

1–10 oz. pkg. spinach, fresh
1/4 t. salt

Drain well. This should be 3/4 c. spinach, packed down. Place spinach in bowl and chop.

Crumble—do not blend—and mix with spinach:

1 c. Tofu (about 1 cube)

Blend in blender until creamy (1 minute):

1/2 c. cashews, raw
2/3 c. water
1/2 t. onion salt
1/4 t. garlic salt
1/4 t. celery salt
1/4 t. salt or to taste
1 T. Mock Chicken Seasoning #1 (see p119)

Pour blended mixture over spinach and tofu, then add:

2 c. bread crumbs, whole wheat, fresh, lightly packed
or **1 c. oats, quick**

Mix well and shape into patties.
Place in Silverstone frying pan rubbed lightly with oil. Brown on medium-low heat 5 minutes each side.

GARBANZO PATTIES

Mix in a large bowl:

- **2 c. garbanzos, (chick peas), cooked, drained and mashed**
- **3/4 c. water**
- **2/3 c. walnuts, ground**
- **1 t. onion powder**
- **1 T. Mock Chicken Seasoning #2 (see p. 119)**
- **1/4 t. garlic salt**
- **1 c. oats, quick**
- **1 t. Maggi (see p. 2)**
- **1/4 t. sage**
- **1/2 c. bread crumbs, whole grain**

Mix well and form into patties. Fry in non-stick frying pan with a trickle of oil.

SUNFLOWER SEED LOAF

In large bowl:

- **1 stalk celery, chopped fine**
- **1 sm. onion, chopped fine**
- **1/2 c. sunflower seeds, ground**
- **2/3 c. walnuts, ground**
- **2 med. potatoes, raw, peeled and grated** (about 1-3/4 c.)
- **1/2 t. celery salt**
- **1 c. soymilk**
- **1/2 t. onion salt**
- **1/2 t. garlic salt**
- **2 t. Maggi (see p. 2)**
- **1 c. bread crumbs, fresh, pack down lightly**

Mix well and pour into greased Pyrex loaf dish. Cover and bake 50 minutes at 350° F.

Remove cover and bake an additional 10 minutes.

BARLEY BURGERS

In pot: **3 c. water**
1/4 t. salt

Bring to boil.

Add: **1 c. pot (hulled) barley** (don't use pearl barley)

Bring to boil again then lower heat and simmer 1 hour. Turn off heat and let cool on burner. (Keep extra barley for soup.)

Sauté in 1 t. oil and 1 T. water:

1 stalk celery, chopped very fine
1 med.-lg. onion, chopped fine
1/4 t. salt

In large bowl combine:

2 c. barley, cooked
1/2 t. sage
1/4 t. rosemary
1/2 t. garlic salt
1 t. onion powder
1-3/4 c. oats, quick
2/3 c. walnuts, ground
1/4 t. celery salt
1 T. Bisto (see p. 1)
1 T. Maggi (see p. 2)
1/4 t. thyme
1 T. Engevita yeast (see p. 2)
1/4 t. salt
1 T. parsley, fresh chopped, fine
1-1/2 c. water, warm, and dissolve **1 t. Marmite** *or* **Savorex** in it

Mix well and form in burgers. May seem soft but they firm up. Fry with a trickle of oil on a Silverstone frying pan. (If using electric frying pan—set at 300° F.)

For a fruit meal—omit the onion and celery and powder the parsley flakes in coffee grinder.

Pure air, sunlight, abstemiousness (temperate in all things), rest, exercise, proper diet,...water, trust in divine power—these are the true remedies. The Ministry of Healing, p. 127.

SUNBURGERS

Sauté in 1 T. oil and a little water:

1 c.	**onions**
1 clove	**garlic, fresh**

In medium size pot, add:

4 c.	**water**
1/4 c.	**Maggi (see p. 2)**
1 t.	**thyme**
1/2 t.	**garlic powder**
1 t.	**salt**
2 T.	**Engevita yeast (see p. 2)**
2 t.	**Vegetarian Baco Chips**

Bring to boil.

Add:	**4 c.**	**oats, quick**
	1/2 c.	**sunflower seeds, ground fine**
		sautéed onions and garlic

Mix well and set aside to cool. Form into patties and fry on Silverstone frying pan with a trickle of oil until golden brown. *Optional:* Bake in oven on a cookie sheet.

SAVORY MACARONI

Cook 3 cups macaroni in pot of boiling water, lightly-salted, for 8–10 minutes.

When done—drain, then rinse cooked macaroni in cold water and drain again.

Put cooked macaroni in large casserole.

Add:	**6**	**Pecan patties (see p. 15),** crumbled or cut in small cubes
	1 recipe	**Savory Cream Sauce (see p. 68)**
	1 t.	**Maggi (see p. 2)**
	1 c.	**soymilk**
	1/2 t.	**garlic salt**

Sauté in 1 t. oil and 1 T. water or more if needed:

1 med.-lg.	**onion, chopped fine**
4 stalks	**celery, chopped fine**
1/4 t.	**salt**

Stir gently—heat and eat.

MACARONI AND CASHEW PIMENTO CHEESE

Cook macaroni to equal 8 cups cooked.
Rinse with cold water.

Add: **1 recipe Cashew Pimento Cheese Sauce (see p. 65)**

Rinse blender with:

1/4 c. additional water

Add: **1/2 t. salt**

Mix well. Place in casserole.
Bake at 350° F. for 45 minutes or until heated through.

TASTY MACARONI

Cook **macaroni** to equal 8 cups cooked.
Rinse with cold water.
In large flat Pyrex or casserole dish, add:

macaroni
1/2 t. salt

Make and add:

1 recipe Spaghetti Sauce (see p. 68)

In Silverstone frying pan crumble:

6 Pecan Patties (see p. 15)

Fry until crispy.
Add to the above mixture:

1 t. Maggi (see p. 2)

Mix well.
Trickle or cover top with Cashew Pimento Cheese (see p. 65).
Bake at 350° F.

Note: If serving the next day, don't bake or add the cheese. If the macaroni seems a little stiff, add a little water and stir gently with fork. Add Cashew Pimento Cheese on top. Bake at 350° F. for 30–45 minutes until heated through and serve. A dish you can do a day ahead when company is coming.

TASTY STROGANOFF

Sauté lightly in 1 T. oil—add a little water if necessary:

2 med. onions, chopped fine
2 stalks celery, sliced crosswise
1/4 t. salt

In small pot:

1-1/2 c. water
1 c. Walnut Wheat Crumbles (see p. 38)
4 t. Bisto (see p. 1)
1/2 t. garlic salt

Simmer 5 minutes, stir then put on lid and remove from heat. In Silverstone frying pan, add a trickle of oil and heat:

2 c. tofu, firm and cut in 1/2" slices (about 2 cubes)

Sprinkle over tofu slices:

2 t. Bisto (see p. 1)
1 t. Maggi (see p. 2)

Fry 5 minutes, turn over.
Sprinkle **2 t. Bisto** (see p. 1) and **1 t. Maggi** (see p. 2) evenly over tofu slices on other side.

Cut each slice in 6 little cubes. Remove from heat and leave in frying pan.

Blend in blender until creamy:

1/2 c. cashews
1/2 c. water
1/4 t. onion salt
salt to taste

Just before serving combine all in frying pan with tofu cubes and fold in gently. Last of all add **1 t. Maggi** (see p. 2).

Serve immediately on fluffy brown rice or—half-and-half Lundberg brown and white basmati rice (cook both rices separately and combine after cooking).

It's delicious!
A suggestion: keep a batch of "Walnut Wheat Crumbles" in the refrigerator at all times. They keep for months and are handy for quick recipes.

SPECIAL "CORN PATS"

Make ahead of time:

1 recipe Cashew Pimento Cheese Spread **(see p. 167)**
adding **1 t. paprika**

Cool spread.
Add and fold in:

2 c. tofu, firm, grated
1/4 t. more salt

Place in containers and freeze for 1–2 days.
Suggestion: freeze in 3 c. container.
Thaw.

In bowl: **3 c. thawed mixture**

In small pot:

1 c. water, cold
1/4 t. salt
1/4 c. cornmeal

Cook until thick.
Cool and add to above mixture in bowl.

Add: **1 c. potato, raw and grated** (1 medium potato)
1 sm. onion, chopped fine
1/2 t. sweet basil
1/2 c. oats, quick
2 t. Mock Chicken Seasoning #2 **(see p. 119)**
1/4 c. cornmeal, dry grain

Mix well and fry in Silverstone frying pan with a trickle of oil—7 minutes on each side.

A delicious treat!

SAVORY POPCORN

Pop the corn as usual. Season with onion salt, garlic salt and Engevita yeast (see p. 2).

TOFU CORN PUFFS

Blend until creamy in blender (1 minute):

1/2 c. cashews, raw
1/2 c. water

Add and blend:

1 c. tofu, well drained (about 1 cube)
2-1/2 t. Mock Chicken Seasoning #1 (see p. 119)
2 T. dried onion flakes
2 T. water
1 t. onion salt
2 T. Engevita yeast (see p. 2)

Put blended mixture in bowl and stir in:

2 c. corn, cooked and salted
1/4 t. sweet basil
2 c. bread crumbs, whole wheat, fresh

Brown patties on medium-low heat in Silverstone fry pan in a trickle of oil—6 minutes each side.

TAMALE PIE

Mix lightly and thoroughly in large bowl:

3-3/4 c. corn, cooked, lightly-salted
1-3/4 c. tomatoes, canned and salted
1/4 t. garlic powder
1/2 t. onion salt
1/2 c. cashew *or* soy milk
1 c. cornmeal
1/4 t. sweet basil
1/4 t. celery salt
1/4 t. salt

Place in casserole. Bake at 350° F. for 1 hour. Garnish top with sautéed green pepper and Pimento Cheese Sauce (see p. 65).

Bake 5 minutes longer. If serving next day, add green pepper and Pimento Cheese Sauce during last 10 minutes of reheating time.

PIZZA BREAD DRESSING

Spread slices of whole wheat bread with Pimento Cheese Spread (see p. 167). Place another slice on top. Cut into cubes. Place cubes in casserole. Cover with Parmigiana Sauce (see p. 12). Pour Cashew Pimento Cheese Sauce (see p. 65) to taste over top. Add kidney beans to taste. Bake in 350° F. oven for 30 minutes.

SPANISH RICE

Sauté in 1 T. oil:

3/4 c. green pepper, chopped very fine (1/2 large pepper)
1/4 t. salt

Add:

4 c. tomatoes, canned
1/8 t. oregano
1/4 t. celery salt
1/4 t. onion salt
3/4 t. basil
1/4 t. garlic salt
1 t. honey, liquid
2 T. Cashew Pimento Cheese (see p. 65)
1/4 c. Hunt's Tomato paste

Simmer about 10 minutes until flavors are well-blended. In casserole:

3 c. brown rice
3 c. white rice
or **6 c. brown rice**
1/2 c. Cashew Pimento Cheese—*without thickener*
2-1/2 c. above tomato mixture

Optional: **1/4 t. salt**

Mix well. Place in casserole and bake at 350° F. for 35–45 minutes or until well heated through.

Note: Keep the remainder of above sauce (for another day) and add (one or a combination of the following) garbanzos, black beans (see p. 39) or beans of choice. Serve on fluffy brown rice.

CORN BREAD AND BEANS

Cut a square of corn bread (see p. 154)in half.
Pour a ladle of soupy beans over it.
The bean broth may be thickened a little if desired.
This is an all-time favorite!

TASTY MEXICALLI LOAF

Sauté lightly in 1 t. oil and 1 T. water:

1/2 lg. green pepper, chopped fine
1/8 t. salt

Place in bowl:

2 c. tomatoes, whole and juice (canned)
1/8 t. oregano
1/4 t. celery salt
1/4 t. onion salt
3/4 t. sweet basil
1/4 t. garlic powder
1 t. honey, liquid
1 T. Engevita yeast (see p. 2)
1 c. oats, quick
1/3 c. cornmeal
2 c. garbanzos, (chick peas), pureed
1/4 c. water

Mix well and pour in greased Pyrex loaf dish. Cover and bake 45 minutes at 350° F. Remove lid and bake additional 15 minutes.

Delicious for sandwiches. Add chopped black olives.
It sets and slices well after sitting a while.

Courage, hope, faith, sympathy, love, promote health and prolong life. A contented mind, a cheerful spirit, is health to the body and strength to the soul. The Ministry of Healing, *p. 127.*

TO FOO YONG

Blend in blender:

1–10.5 oz tofu, silken, Mori-Nu extra firm
2 T. Maggi (see p. 2)

Sauté in: **2 T. oil** and **1 T. Maggi (see p. 2)**

1 med. onion, chopped
2 c. bean sprouts, fresh, chopped
1 c. snow peas, cut in pieces

Mix together:

4 T. Engevita yeast (see p. 2)
2/3 c. flour, whole wheat
1/2 c. water chestnuts, sliced (approx. 1 small can)
1–10.5 oz tofu, silken, Mori-Nu extra firm

Mix all together. Place 1/3–1/2 cup portions on oiled cookie sheet and shape with spatula about 1/2" thick. Bake at 350° F. for 30 minutes. Turn patties over with spatula and cook an additional 15 minutes.

Sauce:

Mix together in saucepan:

2 c. water, cold
4 T. Maggi (see p. 2)
4 T. cornstarch

Cook over minium high heat until thickened. Serve over top of To Foo Yong. *Thanks Eriann Hullquist for sharing this recipe!*

SWEET AND SOUR PINEAPPLE SAUCE

Drain one 14 oz. can of pineapple tidbits. Measure pineapple juice and add water to equal one cup. Put in small pot:

1 c. pineapple juice and water
2 T. honey, liquid (light)
1 T. lemon juice, fresh

take a small portion of the above liquid and mix with:

1 T. arrowroot powder *or* **cornstarch**

Mix all together, heat and stir until thick, Fold in drained pineapple chunks. Take off burner and set aside.

FRIED RICE

Sauté in 1 T. oil

	1 med.-lg.	**onion, chopped fine**
	1 stalk	**celery, chopped fine**
	1/4 t.	**salt**
	1 T.	**water**
Add:	**4 c.**	**brown rice, cooked, lightly-salted**
	1/2 c.	**green peas, frozen**
	1 T.	**Maggi (see p. 2)**
		Mock Chicken Seasoning #2 to taste (see p. 119)
		salt to taste

Optional: Add Tofu Chick (see p. 18) cut in small pieces.

CHOP SUEY

Prepare vegetables first (washed, cut, diced, etc.).
Set electric frying pan at 325° F.:

	1 T.	**oil**
	1 med.-lg.	**onion, chopped fine**
	2 lg. stalks	**celery, cut thin diagonally**
	1/4 t.	**salt**

Add 1/2 c. water and cover with lid—simmer 3 minutes.

Add:	**2 c.**	**bean sprouts, fresh**
	2 c.	**broccoli flowerettes**
	1/4 t.	**garlic salt**
	1/4 c.	**water**

Cover with lid and simmer 2 minutes.

Add:	**1 T.**	**Bisto (see p. 1)**
	1 T.	**Maggi (see p. 2)**
	1/4 t.	**onion salt**

Serve immediately.
Suggested menu: Fried rice (see p. 36), Chop Suey, To Foo Yung (see p. 35), and Sweet and Sour Pineapple Sauce (see p. 35).

HAYSTACKS

For a Fruit Meal

In an individual bowl:

1/4 c. brown rice, cooked
1/3 c. corn chips
1/2 c. kidney beans (heated)

Desired amounts of:

tomato, chopped (1 suggested)
chopped cucumber
olives, chopped
optional: **green pepper** *or* **avocado**

Let each individual: **salt to taste**

Optional dressings: **Soy Mayonnaise (see p. 83)**
or **Cashew Pimento Cheese Sauce (see p. 65)**

For a Vegetable Meal

Use lettuce, celery, green onions, olives, and dressing.

BREAD DRESSING

Sauté in 2 T. oil:

1 lg. onion, chopped fine
1/4 t. salt

Add: **4 c. whole wheat bread** (a couple of days old) **cut in small cubes**
1/4 t. savory
3/4 t. sage
1 c. tofu, firm, cut in small cubes (about 1 cube)
5 t. Mock Chicken Seasoning #2 (see p. 119) in 1/2 c. warm water
1 c. brown rice, cooked, long-grain

Mix well. If you want a drier dressing leave out 1/4 c. water and use 1 t. less Mock Chicken Seasoning. It's nice with Tofu Chick (see p. 18) pieces.

For a fruit meal omit onions and 1/8 t. salt.

Add: **1 t. onion powder**
Optional: **1/4 c. nuts of choice, roasted and chopped**

WALNUT WHEAT CRUMBLES

Blend in blender until creamy:

1 c. walnuts
1 c. water

Add to blender and blend:

1 c. water
1/4 c. onion powder
1 t. celery salt
1 t. garlic salt
1/2 t. salt

Pour above mixture in 2 qt. sauce pan.

Add: **2-1/2 c. water**

Bring to boil.

Add: **2 c. bulgar wheat (see p. 1)**

Bring to boil. Lower heat to lowest heat for approximately 15 minutes. Let cool till reconstituted.

Pour evenly on 2 Silverstone cookie sheets to dehydrate and dry out at 200° F. for 3-1/2 hours. Turn off oven and thoroughly cool. (Will be dry and crunchy.) Every hour take a fork and fluff or crumble the mixture. Put in jar and keep in refrigerator—it keeps for weeks.

Note: To reconstitute add 1 c. seasoned tomato juice or broth to 2 c. dried mixture of Walnut Wheat Crumbles.

Cook at low heat until reconstituted.
Use in lasagna, chilibeans, stuffed zucchini, on tacos, etc.

COOKING BEANS

QUICK START METHOD

Sort carefully: **2-1/4 c. dry beans (1 lb.)**

Wash with cold water and drain.

In a large pot add: **beans**
7 c. water

Bring to full boil. Turn off heat. Let stand for 1 hour or more. *Optional:* change water, adding 5 cups fresh water.

continued...

Bring to boil, then lower heat, simmer until almost done.
Season: **salt to taste**

For fruit meals: Use less salt and some garlic and onion salts. Continue cooking until the flavor is in the beans and beans are done.

For vegetable meals: Add onion, celery, garlic while cooking, then season with salt when beans are done.

OVERNIGHT METHOD

Sort carefully and wash: **1 lb. dry beans**
Cover with twice as much water and soak overnight.
In the morning, drain beans.
In a large pot, add: **soaked beans** (1 lb.)
7 c. water

Bring to boil, then lower heat to simmer. When almost done, season with salt to taste.
Use this method for soybeans and garbanzos.
Suggestion: For softer soybeans and garbanzos—soak overnight. Drain well and freeze in 1 lb. packages. Thaw when ready to use and proceed as "ready to cook".

BLACK BEANS

Clean, wash and soak beans overnight:

1 lb. black beans

or

Quick Start:
Clean, wash and cover beans with 6 c. water.
Bring to boil, then turn off stove leaving pot on the burner for an hour or longer.

Throw water off and add 5 c. fresh water.
Bring to boil, then lower heat to simmer for 1-1/2 hours. Stir occasionally.

Add: **3/4 t salt**
1/4 t. garlic salt
1/4 t. onion salt

Simmer 30 more minutes or until tender.

Optional: **1 bay leaf**
onion, chopped and **garlic, crushed** for vegetable meal

GARDEN "GREEN SOYBEANS"

Pick the pods when filled out, yet still green and succulent. For the best flavor and nutrient value use as soon after picking as possible.

Wash pods thoroughly to remove the grit and dirt in the fuzzy surface. Cook in boiling water, enough to cover the beans until the beans slip out of the pod easily.

To each pint of shelled soybeans add:

1 c. water
1/2 t. salt
1/4 t. onion salt

Bring to boil, then lower temperature to medium boil and cook 10 minutes. When done, soybeans will be firm with a nutty flavor. To serve, drain liquid from beans (and keep liquid for desired use). Eat the Garden "Green Soybeans" plain, or in a tomato sauce. Soybeans may be used in salads, as baked soybeans or in like manner as other soybeans are used. Garden "Green Soybeans" are very nutritious; rich in vitamins, calcium, iron, and phosphorous.

ROMANO "SHELL OUTS"

Let the Romano green beans get plump and big on the vine in the garden. Let them dry, then "shell out". Cook until tender in a little water.

Season with salt, onion salt, and a little garlic salt. They are delicious and freeze well.

BEAN CROCK "BAKED BEANS"

Rich flavour.
Clean and wash:

2 c. pea beans *or* **navy beans** *or* **great northern beans**

Put washed beans in bean crock and add:

3 c. water

Bake in 300° F. oven for 1 hour.

continued...

Add: **2 c. tomatoes, canned**
1 c. water
1/4 c. molasses, fancy light

Bake at 300° F. for 2-1/2 hours.

Add: **1 c. water**

Bake at 300° F. for 1-1/2 hours with lid off.

Add: **1 t. onion powder**
1/2 t. garlic salt
1/4 t. celery salt
3/4 t. salt

Mix well.
Turn oven to 250° F. Bake 1-1/2 hours longer with lid on or until your beans are done. Different beans take different times—also, it depends on how old the beans are. Add more water only if very thick. If beans seem "soupy" remember they thicken as they sit. *Happy eating!*

HAWAIIAN BAKED BEANS

Sort and clean:

1-1/2 c. dry "white pea beans" *or* **"great northern beans"**

Wash well and cover with 3 or 4 c. water. Soak overnight. In the morning drain and add 3 c. water.
Bring to a boil and simmer until not quite done (3/4–1 hour). Add water, if needed, while simmering. If too watery, use juice for soup. Different beans take more or less water. Drain beans.

Place beans in casserole dish and add:

1 can (14 oz.) pineapple, crushed, unsweetened and juice
8 oz. tomato juice
1/2 t. garlic salt
1/2 t. onion salt
2 T. + 1 t. molasses
1/2 t. salt
1 t. Maggi (see p. 2)

Mix well. Set oven at 300° F. Cover casserole with lid and bake 2 hours or until done. Stir occasionally. Turn off stove and let cool in oven.

BLACK-EYE "PEA" ROAST

1 c. of black-eye peas soaked overnight and cooked the following day. When cooked—blend in blender with 1 cup bean liquid. (Lightly salt when almost done.)

Cook the beans with extra water—hoping to have 1 cup of liquid—but if you don't have quite enough, add water to equal 1 cup.

Add:
- **2 c.** **oats, quick**
- **1/2 c.** **walnuts, ground**
- **1 med.** **onion, chopped fine**
- **1 *or* 2 stalks** **celery, chopped fine**
- **1/2 c.** **soymilk**
- **2 T.** **Bisto (see p. 1)**
- **1/4 t.** **thyme**
- **1/4 t.** **sage**
- **1/4 t.** **garlic powder**
- **1 t.** **salt or to taste**

Mix well and pour into a greased loaf pan and bake at 350° F. for 45 minutes with lid on. Remove cover last 15 minutes of baking.

Thanks Dora Doucette for sharing recipe!

CHILI BEANS

Sauté:
- **1** **green pepper, chopped fine**
- **1 T.** **oil**
- **1/4 c.** **water**
- **1/4 t.** **salt**
- **1/4 t.** **onion powder**

When cooked, add:
- **3 c.** **pinto beans, lightly-salted**
- **3 c.** **kidney beans, lightly-salted**
- **2 c.** **tomato juice**
- **1 T.** **garlic powder**
- **2 T.** **onion powder**
- **2 t.** **paprika**

continued...

1-1/2 c. Walnut Wheat Crumbles (see p. 38)
reconstituted with:
3/4 c. water
3/4 c. tomato juice
2 t. cumin
1/2 t. oregano
1 t. Lorraine's "Italian Seasoning" (see p. 120)
salt to taste

Heat and simmer a few minutes and eat.
Serve with fluffy brown rice.

DAD'S FAVORITE BEANS

Sort carefully—**1 lb. great Northern** *or* **white kidney beans**
Wash well—drain, then soak overnight in twice as much water as beans. In the morning—drain the beans.

In a large pot, simmer: **drained beans**
7 c. water

When almost done add:

desired amount of potatoes, peeled and cut lengthwise in half

Salt to taste and continue cooking until potatoes are done.
Do not overcook.

Serve potatoes with soupy beans. (Add a little water if needed). They taste good together.

Suggested menu: greens or broccoli and tossed salad (see p. 79) with dressing.

A merry (rejoicing) heart doeth good like a medicine.
Proverbs 17:22 KJV.

CHILI BEANS IN-A-HURRY

In a big pot, sauté in 1 T. oil:

1 med. green pepper, chopped fine (3/4 c.)

Add:

4 c. tomatoes, canned
1/8 t. oregano
1/4 t. celery salt
1/4 t. onion salt
3/4 t. sweet basil
1/4 t. garlic powder
1 t. honey, liquid (if tomatoes are tart—add honey to taste)
2 T. Engevita yeast (see p. 2)
1/4 c. Hunt's tomato paste

Reconstitute bulgar wheat in small pot:

2/3 c. water, boiling
1/3 c. bulgar wheat (see p. 1)

Lower heat to lowest temperature and simmer 10 minutes. Add reconstituted bulgar wheat to above sauce.

Add:

2 c. kidney beans, drained (19 oz. can or homecooked)
2 c. garbanzos (chick peas), drained
2 c. lentils, drained

Mix all together. Heat and serve over fluffy brown rice.

Suggestions:

1. Cook beans and freeze in containers —in case of emergency.
2. If you like the seasoning "cumin", add 1 t. instead of sweet basil.

Nothing tends more to promote health of body and of soul than does a spirit of gratitude and praise. The Ministry of Healing, p. 251.

GREEN SPLIT PEA PATTIES

Estonian "rohelise hernc" Kotletid.

Rinse and drain **2 c. dry green split peas** in a big pot.

Add: **6 c. water**

Bring to boil—and turn off heat. Watch carefully—it easily boils over. Let stand 1 hour.

Bring to boil second time—then lower heat to simmer.
Boil 1 hour.
Add and mix well:

1/2 t. salt
2-1/2 t. marjoram
1-1/2 t. sage
1 t. onion salt

Sauté **1 lg. onion** in 1 T. oil.
Add to above mixture.
Put in large bowl.

Add: **3/4 c. walnuts, ground**
1 c. soymilk (liquid)
2 c. oats, quick
1 "Shredded Wheat" (cereal), crumbled fine

Mix well and shape into patties. If hands get too sticky, dip in bowl of water. The patties may seem soft but they firm up while frying. Fry on a Silverstone frying pan with a trickle of oil. Makes 3 dozen patties.

RICE IN A SKILLET

In Silverstone frying pan:

6 c. brown rice, cooked
1 c. green peppers, chopped fine
2 c. garbanzos (chick peas), drained
(19 oz. can or homecooked)

Season with Mock Chicken Seasoning #2 (see p. 119).
Heat and eat.
A *Summer Quickie:* serve cold with Soy Mayonnaise (see p. 83).
Optional: Add 1/2 c. sliced olives and 1/4 c. pimento, chopped.

"GARBANZO" BURGERS

"Old Vegetarian Pattie" Recipe

Wash and soak overnight:

1/2 c. garbanzos (chick peas), dried

Sauté in 1 t. oil + 2 T. water:

1 med.-lg. onion, chopped fine

Put the sautéed onions in a big bowl.

Add: **2 c. oats, quick**

Blend in blender until creamy:

the soaked garbanzos (1 cup)
1 c. water

Add: **1/2 c. soymilk**
1/2 t. garlic salt
1/2 t. celery salt
1/2 t. onion salt
1/4 t. sage
1 T. Maggi (see p. 2)

Pour creamy mixture over oats and onions in bowl.

Add: **2/3 c. walnuts, ground**

Mix well. Let stand 5 minutes for oats to absorb liquid. Fry patties on Silverstone frying pan at 300° F. with a trickle of oil. Drop mixture by large tablespoonsful. Fry 6–7 minutes on each side.

Note: To reheat—put in Pyrex dish and cover so they won't dry out. Serve with Brown Gravy.

"CHICK" GRAVY WITH GARBANZOS

1 recipe "Chick" Gravy (see p. 65)

Fold in: **2 c. garbanzos (chick peass), drained, cooked and lightly-salted**

Serve on fluffy brown rice.

SAVORY GARBANZOS

Sauté in 1 T. oil:

1/2 *or* 1 green pepper, whole, chopped fine
1/4 t. salt

Add:

2 c. tomatoes, canned
1/2 t. onion salt
1/4 t. celery seed
1/2 t. sweet basil
4 c. garbanzos (chick peas), cooked, drained and lightly-salted
2 t. honey, liquid
1/2 t. garlic powder

Thicken with 1 T. cornstarch dissolved in a little water. Serve over fluffy brown rice.

PINTO-BRAZILIAN PATTIES

Sauté in 1 t. oil and 1 T. water

1 med. onion, chopped fine
1 stalk celery, chopped fine
1/8 t. salt

Add above to a big bowl.

Add: **2-1/2 c. pinto beans, cooked, soupy, lightly-salted and blended until creamy**

Add:

1/2 c. Brazil nuts, ground
1/4 t. marjoram
1/4 t. sweet basil
1/4 t. sage
1-1/2 c. oats, quick
1 t. Maggi (see p. 2)
1/4 t. celery salt
1/4 t. garlic salt

Mix well. Shape into patties and fry on a Silverstone frying pan with a trickle of oil. Serve with a gravy or Tofu Sour Cream (see p. 85).

LARGE LIMAS

Clean and wash **1 lb. large dry limas**.
Place in large pot and add: **6 c. water**
Bring to boil and simmer approximately 1 hour.

Season: **1/2 t. garlic salt**
1/2 t. salt or to taste

Optional: For vegetable meal sauté 2 onions and add to beans. For fruit meal—Instead of 6 c. water, add 4 c. water + 2 c. tomato juice. For last half hour of cooking, add 1/2 to 1 green pepper (chopped fine) and, if desired, 1 to 3 level T. molasses to taste.

PINTO-LENTILS

Sauté in 1 t. oil and 1 T. water:

1 med. green pepper, chopped
season with onion and garlic salt to taste

Add equal amounts of:

1-1/2 c. pinto beans, cooked
1-1/2 c. lentils, seasoned

Mix lightly. Heat and serve on fluffy brown rice.
For Vegetable Meal, sauté:

1 lg. onion
2 cloves garlic, minced
1 stalk celery instead of green pepper

SEASONED LENTILS

Clean **1 lb. brown lentils**. Wash well.
Place lentils in a big pot. Add **6 c. water**.
Bring to boil and simmer for 1 hour, stirring occasionally.

Season with:

1/2 t. garlic salt
1/2 t. onion salt
1/4 t. celery salt

COMPANY LENTIL LOAF

In bowl combine:

2 c.	**Seasoned Lentils (see p. 48), drained**
2/3 c.	**walnuts, ground**
1/4 c.	**tomato juice**
1/2 c.	**water**
1/2 c.	**soymilk *or* nutmilk**
1 t.	**Maggi (see p. 2)**
1 T.	**Bisto (see p. 1)**
1/2 t.	**garlic powder**
1/2 t.	**onion powder**
1/4 t.	**salt**
1/4 t.	**celery salt**
1 c.	**oats, quick**
1/2 t.	**sage**
1	**"Shredded Wheat" (cereal), finely crumbled**

Mix well and place in greased loaf pan.
Cover and bake at 350° F. for 45 minutes.
Remove lid and bake an additional 15 minutes. Then cover until ready to serve.

MOTHER'S LENTIL PATTYCAKES

Sauté in 1 T. oil:	1 med.	**onion, chopped fine**
	1/8 t.	**salt**
Combine in bowl:		**sautéed onions**
	1 c.	**mashed potato, lightly-salted**
	2/3 c.	**walnuts, ground**
	1/2 c.	**soymilk or nutmilk**
	1 c.	**Seasoned Lentils, drained (see p. 48)**
	1 c.	**oats, quick**
	1 t.	**Maggi (see p. 2)**
	1/4 t.	**sage**
	1/4 t.	**garlic salt**
	1/4 t.	**celery salt**

Mix well. Let stand for 5 minutes.
Shape into patties and dip in crumbs. Fry in Silverstone frying pan with trickle of oil.

Thanks Mom for sharing recipe!

LENTIL "MEATBALLS" OR "PATTIES"

Sauté in sauce pan:

	1 T.	**oil**
	1 med.	**onion, chopped very fine**
	3 cloves	**garlic, chopped very fine**
	1/8 t.	**salt**
Add:	1-1/2 c.	**lentil broth** (from Seasoned Lentils recipe on p. 48)
	1 c.	**lentils, drained and cooked**
	1 c.	**Walnut Wheat Crumbles (see p. 38)**

Pour in bowl to cool.

Add:	1/4 t.	**sage**
	1/4 t.	**onion salt**
	1/2 c.	**oats, quick**
	1 c.	**bread crumbs, soft whole wheat** *or* sufficient to shape into meatballs
	2 t.	**Maggi (see p. 2)**
	1 t.	**Bisto (see p. 1)**
	1/2 c.	**walnuts, ground**

Fry in Silverstone frying pan with a trickle of oil until golden.

LENTIL LOAF

In large bowl:

1 med.-lg.	**onion, chopped fine**
2 stalks	**celery, chopped fine (1 c.)**
2 c.	**lentils, cooked and drained**
1 c.	**tofu, crumbled**
3/4 c.	**walnuts, ground**
1 c.	**soymilk**
1/2 t.	**sage**
2 T.	**Mock Chicken Seasoning #2 (see p. 119)**
1 t.	**Maggi (see p. 2)**
1/2 t.	**garlic salt**
1/4 t.	**onion salt**
1/4 t.	**celery salt**
1/4 t.	**salt**
2	**"Shredded Wheat" (cereal), crumbled fine**

continued...

Mix well and bake in covered, greased loaf pan or Pyrex dish.

Bake at 350° F. for 45 minutes. Remove lid. Bake additional 15 minutes.

Turn off oven and let set 10–15 minutes longer. Then put on lid or serve.

LENTIL PECAN LOAF

Sauté in 1 T. oil:

1 stalk celery, chopped fine
1 med.-lg. onion, chopped fine

Put above in bowl and add:

1-1/2 c. lentils, cooked, lightly-salted and drained
1-1/4 c. tofu, crumbled (about 1 cube)
1-1/2 c. brown rice, cooked and lightly-salted
1-1/4 c. soymilk
1/2 c. oats, quick
1/2 c. pecans, ground
1/4 c. walnuts, ground
3/4 t. salt
2 t. Maggi (see p. 2)
2 T. Mock Chicken Seasoning #1 (see p. 119)
1 T. Mock Chicken Seasoning #2 (see p. 119)
1/4 t. sage

Mix well. Pour in greased Pyrex loaf dish. Bake covered for 1 hour at 350° F.

SAVORY LENTIL SPROUTS

Sauté onion and celery. When almost done, add lentil sprouts with couple of tablespoons of water.

Bring to a boil and thicken with a little cornstarch if you want them thicker.

Season with salt, garlic salt and a dash of Maggi (see p. 2).

SAVORY LENTIL STEW

Cook in saucepan for 45 minutes:

	2 c.	**green lentils, washed**
	8 c.	**water**
	1	**bay leaf**

Remove bay leaf.

Add:	**1 med.**	**onion, chopped fine**
	1 c.	**celery, sliced** (2 stalks)
	1 clove	**garlic, minced**
	1 t.	**garlic salt or to taste**
	3/4 t.	**salt**
	1/8 t.	**oregano**
	3	**carrots, cut in large pieces**
	4 med.	**potatoes, diced**

Cook additional 45 minutes or until done and serve.

OR

After adding carrots and potatoes, bake in oven until done.

ESAU'S POTTAGE

Bring **4 c. water** to boil in pot.
Add and stir: **1/3 c. uncooked brown rice**

	1/2 t.	**salt**
	1 c.	**dry lentils, cleaned and washed**
	1 T.	**onion powder**
	1/4 t.	**celery salt**
	1/2 t.	**garlic powder**
Optional:	**1**	**bay leaf**

Simmer for almost 1 hour.

LEFT OVER ESAU'S POTTAGE

Add: **peanut butter to taste**
a little sage

continued...

Form into croquettes and roll in seasoned crumbs.

Heat in 350° F. oven for 15–20 minutes until heated. Don't let them dry out in oven.

Suggested menu: Croquettes, sweet potatoes, broccoli, tossed salad.

LENTIL STROGANOFF

Sauté in 1 T. oil and a little water, if needed:

1 c. onion, chopped fine
2 stalks celery, sliced in thin slices
1 clove garlic, minced
1/4 t. salt

Add: **2-1/2 c. lentils, lightly-salted and drained**

Blend in blender: **1/2 c. cashews**
1/2 c. water

As it gets thick add:

1/4 c. more water
1 T. Mock Chicken Seasoning #2 (see p. 119)
salt to taste

Combine all. Heat and serve over fluffy brown rice.

SPANISH LENTILS

Cook Seasoned Lentils (see p. 48). Drain and keep broth for soup.

Fold in desired amount of Spaghetti Sauce (see p. 68).

SPANISH BABY LIMAS OR ANY BEANS

Cook beans according to directions on package. Season lightly with salt. Drain and keep broth for soup.

Fold in desired amount of Spaghetti Sauce (see p. 68)—generally 1 recipe Spaghetti Sauce.

Serve on fluffy brown rice.

RED LENTIL PATTIES

Sort, clean and wash **1 c. red lentils.**
Put lentils in a big pot.

Add:	**2-1/2 c.**	**water**
	1/2 t.	**celery salt**
	1/2 t.	**garlic salt**
	1/2 t.	**onion salt**

Bring to boil and simmer 15 minutes. Turn off heat and let cool. Add seasoned, cooked red lentils in a big bowl.

Add:	**1 c.**	**oats, quick**
	1/4 t.	**sage**
	1/4 t.	**sweet basil**
	1/4 t.	**thyme**
	1 c.	**bread crumbs, fresh, lightly packed**
	1/4 t.	**salt**
	1/2 c.	**walnuts, ground**

Mix well. Wet hands a little then shape into patties. Fry on Silverstone frying pan with a trickle of oil. They will seem very soft but they firm up the longer they stand.

RED LENTILS "POTTAGE"

Clean, sort and wash well:

2 c. **dry, red lentils**

Place in saucepan:

lentils, washed
4 c. **water**

Bring to boil, then simmer for 1/2 hour.
Sauté in 1 T. olive oil and 2 T. water:

4 cloves	**garlic, minced**
2 med.	**onions, chopped fine**
1/4 t.	**salt**

When done, add onion mixture to cooked lentils.

Add:	**1 t.**	**garlic powder**
	3/4 t.	**salt**

Suggested menu: Serve Red Lentils "Pottage" over fluffy brown rice with greens, or broccoli and salad.

CRUNCHY PEANUT PATTIES

In pot:

3 c. water, cold
1/4 t. salt
3/4 c. cornmeal

Bring to boil, stirring constantly.
Lower to simmer for 15 minutes on lowest heat setting.
Put cooked cornmeal in a big bowl.
Sauté in 1 T. oil:

3/4 c. celery, chopped fine
1 med.-lg. onion, chopped fine
1/4 t. salt

Add to above mixture:

2 c. pinto beans, cooked, lightly-salted, drained and mashed
1/2 c. peanut butter, crunchy
1/2 t. celery salt
1/2 t. garlic salt
1 t. onion salt
1/2 t. sweet basil
1/2 t. marjoram
1/2 t. thyme
1 c. bread crumbs, whole wheat, fresh

Mix well with wet hands and shape into patties. Fry on a Silverstone frying pan with a trickle of oil.

At mealtime do not feel hurried, but eat slowly and with cheerfulness, with your heart filled with gratitude to God for all His blessings. The Ministry of Healing, p. 306.

PEANUT TOMATO LOAF

In large bowl combine:

1/4 c.	**peanut butter**
1 c.	**tomato juice**
1–10 oz. can	**tomato soup**
1 t.	**onion powder**
2 t.	**Mock Chicken Seasoning #2 (see p. 119)**
1 T.	**Bisto (see p. 1)**
1/2 c.	**"Cream of Wheat" dry cereal**
1/2 c.	**Quaker's "oat bran" dry cereal**
1/2 t.	**sage**
1/2 t.	**garlic powder**
	salt to taste

Mix well. Pour into greased casserole.
Bake at 350° F. for 45 minutes or until firm.
Place a small bowl of water in oven while baking.

Thanks Ursula Krahne for sharing recipe!

PEANUT LOAF

Bake a day ahead and reheat for firmer loaf.
In large bowl:

1 c.	**pinto beans (or Romano), cooked, lightly-salted and mashed**
1/2 c.	**peanut butter**
2 c.	**potato water(see note below)**
3 T.	**cornstarch**
1 med.	**onion, chopped fine**
1 lg. stalk	**celery, chopped very fine**
1/4 t.	**sage**
1/2 t.	**garlic salt**
1/4 t.	**onion salt**
1/4 t.	**celery salt**
1 c.	**brown rice, cooked and lightly-salted**

Mix well. Put in greased Pyrex loaf dish and cover. Bake at 350° F. for 45 minutes. Remove lid and bake 45 minutes more or until set. It may be a soft set. The next day it is firmer, and cuts nicely.

continued...

If you want a very firm loaf, add **1/4 c. cornstarch.**

NOTE: Grate 1 medium potato in 1-1/4 c. water. Add 1/4 t. salt and cook for 15 minutes. If not enough water add to equal 2 c. Blend in blender.

Thanks Mom (Mrs. G. R. Nash) for sharing recipe!

SOY SIZZLERS

Soak overnight:

1/2 c. and **2 heaping T. dry soybeans**
(in the morning should be 1-1/4 c. soaked)

Sauté in 1 T. oil:

1 med. **onion, chopped fine**
2 stalks **celery, chopped fine** (about 1 c.)
1 clove **garlic, minced**
1/4 t. **salt**

Blend until creamy in blender:

1-1/4 c. **soybeans, soaked, raw**
1-1/2 c. **water**

Add:
1/4 t. **celery salt**
1/2 t. **garlic salt**
1 T. **Engevita yeast (see p. 2)**
1/8 t **savory**
1/2 t. **thyme**
1/4 t. **marjoram**
1/4 t. **salt**
1 t. **Maggi (see p. 2)**
1 t. **parsley flakes**

Pour liquid mixture into bowl and add:

sautéed onion and celery mixture
1-1/4 c. **oats, quick**
1/2 c. **walnuts, ground**

Mix well and let stand 5 minutes—for oats to absorb liquid. Fry patties in Silverstone frying pan with just a trickle of oil—7 minutes on each side.

DELICIOUS BAKED SOYBEANS

2 c. soybeans, soaked overnight

In the morning, cook until tender. Season with **salt to taste** (about 1 t.). Simmer for 10 minutes longer. Add to drained soybeans:

2 c. **tomatoes, canned**
1 T. **onion powder**
3 T. **molasses**
salt to taste
1 T. **Vegetarian Baco Chips** *or* **Bakon yeast**

Place in casserole and bake in slow oven at 325° F. for 2 hours.

GOLDEN SOYA PATTIES

In a large bowl combine:

3 c. **oats, quick**
2 c. **water, warm**

Blend and puree **2 c. cooked soybeans** (lightly-salted when cooking). Add to above ingredients. Sauté in 1 T. oil and 1 T. water:

1 lg. **onion, chopped fine**
2 cloves **garlic, minced**
1/4 t. **salt**

Add to above ingredients.

Add: **1 T.** **Maggi (see p. 2)**
1 t. **thyme**
1 c. **wheat germ**
1 t. **salt or to taste**

Drop by spoonsful on Silverstone frying pan with a trickle of oil. Fry until golden on each side.

Thanks Rita Chen Brown for sharing recipe!

SPROUTED WHEAT BURGERS

3/4 c. wheat kernels (berries) = 2 c. sprouted wheat.
The sprouts should be no longer than the wheat kernel.

In bowl:

2 c. wheat kernels (berries), sprouted
1/3 c. sunflower seeds, ground
1/3 c. pumpkin seeds, ground
2 c. millet, cooked
2 T. Maggi (see p. 2)
1 T. onion powder
1/4 t. sage
1/2 c. bread crumbs, soft
1/4 t. celery salt
1/2 t. garlic powder
2 T. peanut butter

Shape into patties. Fry in Silverstone frying pan with a little oil. Brown on both sides.

Thanks Ursula Krahne for recipe!

NUTTOSE

Mix well in large bowl:

1 c. peanut butter
1 t. onion powder
2 c. water
1/4 c. arrowroot powder
1 c. brown rice, cooked
1/2 t. salt
1/4 t. celery salt
1/4 t. garlic powder
1/2 t. onion salt
1/2 c. Quaker oat bran cereal
2 t. Mock Chicken Seasoning #2 (see p. 119)

Mix well. Place in 2 greased tins (19 fl. oz.). Cover with wax paper, double thickness, and tie with string. Place foil cover on top of wax paper, molding to tin, and tie with another string. Steam in pan containing enough water so pans will not tip over. Cover and boil for 2-1/2–3 hrs. Allow cans to cool before removing from tins.

QUICKIE CROQUETTES

Mix well in large bowl:

1 c. cornmeal, cooked (see p. 131) cereal (leftover)
1/2 c. mashed potato
1 c. Nuteena *or* **homemade Nuttose (see p. 59)**
1/4 t. sage
Mock Chicken Seasoning #2 (see p. 119) to taste

Form into mini croquettes and roll in toasted bread crumbs with a dash of Mock Chicken Seasoning #2. Heat and serve with Thousand Island Dressing (see p. 84).

SOYBEAN CURD (TOFU)

Recipe yields approximately 2 lbs. curd.

1. Wash 2 cups of dry soy beans and soak overnight.
2. Rinse well. Liquify beans until very smooth—1 part beans to 2–3 parts water.
3. Separate residue from milk (squeeze in cheese cloth, nylon hose or curtain, etc.)
4. Bring milk to boiling point. Stir constantly as milk scorches easily. A pan sprayed with "Pam" doesn't scorch milk as easily.
5. Add 2 t. calcium chloride (purchased from any pharmacy) dissolved in 1/4 cup warm water to milk stirring slowly while adding it. Stir evenly but not too much.
6. Wait 3–5 minutes until milk curdles well. Gently lift curd into cheese cloth. Press into mold and rinse. Let drain well.
7. Put curd in a container filled with cold water. Store in refrigerator.

Used by permission of Gary Strunk. "Taste of Nature" class participation Magazine No. 6.

Thought for the day

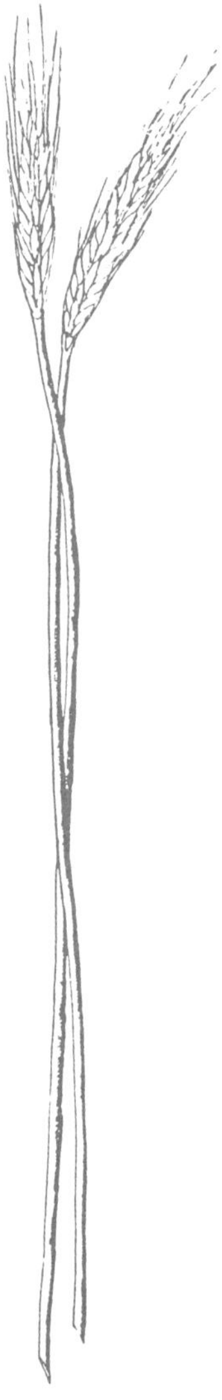

Do you know you are loved?

God says in Jeremiah 31:3 NIV, "I have loved you with an everlasting love...." How much is everlasting? Look at the beauty all around you, the lovely flowers, the tall trees, the warm sunshine, and the singing birds or the gentle snow or falling rain.

Have you ever thought of all the wide variety and assortment of our food? The grains and seeds: oats, wheat, rye, barley, buckwheat, rice, corn, millet, sesame, sunflower, etc. The nuts: walnuts, almonds, pecans, pistachio, cashews, filberts, Brazil nuts, etc. The fruits: oranges, apples, grapes, bananas, cherries, apricots, strawberries, raspberries, pears, watermelons, papaya, and the tropical fruits—all because He loves us. There is also the wide assortment of vegetables.

We have only mentioned a few of the special choices given us by our loving Creator. It is God's way of saying, "I love you. I know your needs. It was I who made you and put the vitamins and minerals and essential elements in the food for your health and happiness." Everyone is precious in Jesus' sight. Remember God says, "I have loved you with an everlasting love."

Notes

Gravies & Sauces

BROWN GRAVY

In small frying pan—sauté in 1 T. oil:

1 sm. onion, chopped very fine

Fry until golden.

Add: **3 T. flour, white unbleached** and mix in with onions.
Add: **1 c. water, cold,** stirring constantly with wire whip.
Add: **1 more c. cold water** *or* **unsalted potato broth** (off potatoes), stirring constantly.
Add: **1 T. Maggi (see p. 2)**
1/2 t. garlic powder

In **2/3 c. additional cold water** mix **2 T. Bisto (see p. 1)**. Add to above ingredients; stirring constantly until thick and creamy.

RICH BROWN GRAVY

Blend in blender till creamy:

1/2 c. cashews
1/2 c. water

Add to blender and blend:

1 c. water
3 T. Bisto (see p. 1)
1 T. Maggi (see p. 2)
2 T. arrowroot
1/2 t. garlic powder
1/2 t. onion salt

Add and quick blend:

2-1/2 c. water

Pour above mixture inpot, and stir constantly until thick.

Add and dissolve **1/2 t. Marmite** *or* **Savorex** to hot gravy

CREAM SAUCE FOR VEGETABLES

Prepare 1/2 recipe of Savory Cream Sauce (see p. 68), omitting Mock Chicken Seasoning and onion salt.

Drain 2 c. cooked vegetables and fold in Cream Sauce.

✗

CASHEW PIMENTO CHEESE SAUCE

Blend in blender till creamy (1 minute):

1 c. cashews, raw
1 c. water
2 T. sesame seeds, unhulled

Add and blend as needed for smooth blending:

1 c. water

Add and blend:

1/4 c. sweet red pepper *or* **pimento** (not pickled),
cut in pieces (if pale add a little more)
3/4 t. salt
1/8 t. celery seed
1/4 t. garlic powder
1/3c – **1/4 c. Engevita yeast (see p. 2)** or nutritional yeast flakes
2 T. lemon juice, fresh
1 t. onion salt

Pour into container. Refrigerate.
Note: See p. 118 on how to freeze red peppers section.

"CHICK" GRAVY

Sauté in 1 t. oil—add 1 t. water:

1 sm. onion, chopped very fine

Blend in blender till creamy:

1 c. "garbanzo (chick pea)" broth
1/2 c. garbanzos (chick peas)
1 t. Mock Chicken Seasoning #2 (see p. 119)

Add: **1 c. water**
2–3 t. arrowroot powder or corn starch
1/4 t. garlic salt
salt to taste

Bring to boil, stirring constantly until thick and creamy. Add onions and serve.

CHICKEN-LIKE GRAVY

Blend in blender till creamy, 1 minute:

1/2 c. cashews
1/2 c. water

Add:

2 c. water
2 c. potato water
2 T. Mock Chicken Seasoning #2 (see p. 119)
1 t. onion salt
2 t. arrowroot powder
1/2 t. celery salt

Blend till mixed. Pour in pot. Bring to boil stirring constantly until thick and creamy. Serve.

GARBANZO GRAVY

Blend in blender till creamy:

1/4 c. cashews, raw, washed
1/4 c. water

Add and blend:

3/4 c. garbanzos (chick peas), cooked and lightly-salted
3/4 c. water

While blending, add:

1-1/2 c. additional water
3/4 t. onion salt
1 t. onion powder
1/2 t. garlic salt
1/2 t. Maggi (see p. 2)
2 t. Mock Chicken Seasoning #2 (see p. 119)
3 t. arrowroot flour

Put in pot, bring to boil and stir constantly till thick and creamy. Serve.

LENTIL GRAVY

Blend in blender:

1-1/2 c. Seasoned Lentils (see p. 48), cooked and drained
1-1/2 c. water
1/4 t. garlic salt
1 T. Mock Chicken Seasoning #2 (see p. 119)
1/4 t. onion salt
2 t. arrowroot powder *or* **cornstarch**

Pour in pot. Bring to boil stirring constantly until gravy is thick and creamy. Remove from burner, leave lid on till ready to serve.

MOCKZARELLA CHEESE SAUCE

Blend in blender till creamy (1 minute):

1-1/2 c. cashews, raw
1-1/2 c. water

Add and blend:

1/2 c. water
3 T. Engevita yeast (see p. 2)
1 t. salt
1 t. onion salt
1/4 c. dried onion flakes
2 T. lemon juice, fresh
1/8 t. garlic salt

Refrigerate till ready to use.

PEANUT BUTTER GRAVY

Blend in blender till smooth:

1/2 c. peanut butter
2 c. water
1/4 c. cornstarch
1/4 t. salt or to taste
1 t. onion powder
1/4 t. celery seed

Pour into pot and bring to boil, stirring constantly until gravy is thick. Serve on fluffy brown rice.

SAVORY CREAM SAUCE

Blend in blender till creamy:

1 c. cashews, raw, washed
1 c. water

Add and blend:

1-1/2 c. water
1/2 t. salt
1/2 t. onion salt
2 t. arrowroot powder
Optional: **2 t. Mock Chicken Seasoning #1 (see p. 119)**

Pour into pot, bring to boil stirring constantly until thick and creamy.

Optional:

(1) To sauce, add 2 c. cooked, salted, drained garbanzos. Delicious over baked potatoes.

(2) Add desired amount Vegetarian Baco Chips—making a "Chip Beef" gravy 1/4–1/2 c.

(3) To Savory Sauce, add frozen green limas, frozen peas and pimento pieces.

SPAGHETTI SAUCE

Sauté in 1 T. oil:

1 med. green pepper, chopped very fine (about 3/4 c.)
1/4 t. salt

Add: **4 c. tomatoes, canned**
1/8 t. oregano
1/4 t. celery salt
1/4 t. onion salt
3/4 t. sweet basil
1/4 t. garlic salt
1 t. honey, liquid (if tomatoes are tart—add honey to taste)
2 T. Cashew Pimento Cheese (see p. 65)
or **1 T. Engevita yeast (see p. 2)**
1/4 c. "Hunts" tomato paste

Simmer about 10 minutes till flavors are well-blended.
Serve over soy noodles or spaghetti.

Thought for the day

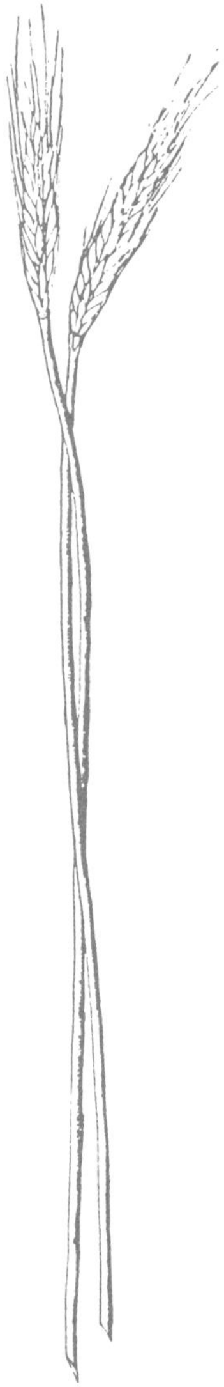

What a joy to listen to God. He talks to us in His word, the Bible. In every promise, "He is speaking to us individually, speaking as directly as if we could listen to His voice. It is in these promises that Christ communicates to us His grace and power.... Nothing else can have such healing power. Nothing besides can impart the courage and faith which give vital energy to the whole being." *Ministry of Healing*, p. 122.

God made wonderful promises to Abraham in the Bible, promising to make him a great nation through which the Messiah was to come, and assuring him that he would have children as the stars in the sky. Yet, year after year, Abraham and Sarah were childless. Abraham even tried to help God out by doing things his own way, to his sorrow. Then when everything looked hopeless, when Abraham was 99 years old, he and Sarah believed God, and Sarah conceived. When things look hopeless, believe God's promises to you. He is faithful.

In Matthew 6:26 Jesus says, "Behold the fowls of the air: for they sow not, neither do they reap, nor gather into barns; yet your heavenly Father feedeth them. Are ye not much better than they?"

God does not forget us for one brief moment. *Ibid.*, p.488.

Remember, God loves you.

Notes

Salads & Dressings

BEAN MEDLEY SALAD

1 c. kidney beans, cooked, seasoned and drained
1 c. green beans, cooked, seasoned and drained
1 c. wax beans, cooked, seasoned and drained
1 c. garbanzos (chick peas), cooked, seasoned and drained

Optional: green lima beans or beans of choice

For fruit meal, add:

1/4 c. green pepper, chopped
1/4 c. red pepper, chopped

Season lightly, if needed, with onion salt (or onion powder) and celery seed.

Marinate with equal amounts of undiluted, sweetened frozen lemonade and oil.

For vegetable meal, add:

green onions
celery, chopped
radishes, sliced thin (add just before eating)

ENDIVE SALAD

Rinse and wash:

1 bunch of endive under HOT water
(This removes some of the bitter taste.)

Remove endive leaves from stem and break in pieces in large bowl.

Cook: **2 c. cubed potatoes** until just done. Season lightly with salt to taste. Drain and keep potato liquid for soup or gravy. Combine potatoes and endive. Season with salt.

DRESSING

In small cup:

3 T. lemon juice
2 T. olive oil
dash of salt
1/4 c. potato water

Mix well. Toss together and serve.

Optional: **2 T. green onion, chopped fine**

CARROT SALAD

Grate in bowl:

3 c. carrots, grated

Add: **1/4 t. salt**

1 stalk celery, washed, sliced in half lengthwise and then sliced thin

Blend in cup and add:

1/3 c. Soy Mayonnaise (see p. 83)

Plus

1 T. pineapple juice

or

1 T. soymilk to dilute

Mix all together gently.

Serve on frilly lettuce leaf in individual salad bowls. Garnish with a sprig of parsley.

CELERY STUFFED

Wash celery and let stand in a little water to keep crisp in the refrigerator.

Just before serving fill with Mockzarella Cheese Sauce (see p. 67), or peanut butter or Tofu Spread (see p. 172).

CORN SALAD

In bowl:

1–12 oz. can Green Giant corn, drained
1/2 t. onion powder
1/4 t. celery salt
2-3 T. green pepper, chopped
2-3 T. red bell pepper, chopped
1 T. olive oil or less
1 T. lemon juice
1/4 t. sweet basil
a little dill weed *or* fresh dill

Mix well and serve.

CREAMY CUCUMBER SALAD

Just before serving, slice or dice cucumbers in bowl. Salt to taste.

Add Creamy Dressing for Cucumbers (see p. 81).
Mix well and serve immediately.
Optional: Add a little red or green bell pepper, chopped fine, for color.

GRAPE SALAD (an individual salad)

On bread and butter plate:

1/2 pear, rounded side up (large canned pears)

Frost with thick, creamy Almond Butter (see p. 172).
Wash seedless grapes and cut in half lengthwise.
Cover frosted pear with halves of grapes (round side up) to resemble a bunch of grapes.

Cut a mini grape leaf from a green pepper to garnish salad or use a real grape leaf, if available. Chill in refrigerator till ready to eat. Serve with a fruit meal.

LETTUCE SALAD WITH TOASTED SESAME SEEDS (a favorite)

In bowl:

1/2 head lettuce, broken in pieces
3 *or* 4 T. sesame seeds, toasted*
3 or 4 green onions, sliced thin
salt to taste

In small bottle:

2 T. oil
2 T. lemon juice
1/16 t. salt

Shake and pour on salad. Toss and serve.
Optional: a little spinach for color
* Toast unhulled sesame seeds in a 300° F. oven for 10 minutes. Do extra to have on hand and store in a bottle.

Delicious in salads or cereals.

MACARONI SALAD

Mix in a large bowl:

6 c. macaroni, cooked, salted, rinsed and drained
2 c. cucumber, diced
1/2 c. green pepper, chopped
1/2 c. olives, sliced
1/3 c. pimento, chopped
1/4 t. celery salt
1/2 t. onion salt
1/2 t. dried dill weed, powdered *or* **fresh dill to taste**
2/3 c. Soy Mayonnaise (see p. 83)

Chill till ready to serve.

POTATO SALAD

Cook until tender:

8 med. potatoes

Peel potatoes and dice in small cubes.
Place in bowl, add and mix:

1-1/4 c. celery, chopped fairly fine
4 green onions including stems, chopped very fine
3/4 c. Soy Mayonnaise (see p. 83)—or enough to moisten
1/2 c. radishes, chopped fine
salt to taste

Chill and serve.

ROYAL BEET SALAD

Boil beets till tender, drain and cool.
Peel beets, dice in small cubes.
Add salt to taste.
Add Soy Mayonnaise (see p. 83) to taste.
Place on frilly lettuce leaf.

Optional: Add 1 or 2 sliced green onions.

SPINACH SALAD

Toss in bowl:

- **2-1/2 c. spinach, crisp and washed**—tear in bite-sized pieces
- **2-1/2 c. lettuce, prepared as spinach**
- **1** *or* **2 stalks celery, cut in two and sliced thin if a large stalk.** If smaller, just slice thin.
- **5 radishes, sliced thin**

Serve with lemon juice dressing to taste:

- **1/3 c. lemon juice**
- **1/4 c. olive** *or* **salad oil**
- **1/2 t. salt**

Optional: **1 T. onion, freshly grated**

SPRINGTIME CABBAGE SALAD

In large bowl:

- **1 sm. head cabbage, shredded**
- **1/2 c. radishes, sliced**
- **1/2 to 1 c. parsley, finely snipped**
- **2 c. green peas, frozen, thawed** (not cooked)
- **1/2 t. salt**
- **6 green onion tops, sliced**

Mix all ingredients and cover. Refrigerate till ready to use. Mix with Soy Mayonnaise (see p. 83) thinned with a little soymilk. Garnish with radish roses and sprigs of parsley.

SOYBEAN SALAD (OR BEAN OF CHOICE)

- **2 c. soybeans, cooked that have been seasoned while cooking. drained well.**
- **3/4 c. celery, chopped fine**
- **green onions to taste**
- **carrot, grated** (small amount)

Just before serving, mix in Soy Mayonnaise (see p. 83) to taste. Serve on a lettuce leaf and garnish with parsley.

STUFFED TOMATO

Cut tomato as desired.
Stuff with Tofu Cottage Cheese. (see p. 78)
Add green pepper chopped in small cubes for color to the Tofu Cottage Cheese if desired.

Place stuffed tomato on green pepper rings, cucumber slices or alfalfa sprouts.

TEBULA (COUS COUS OR USE SAME RECIPE WITH BULGAR WHEAT)

Reconstitute cous cous:

3 c. water
1/4 t. salt

When water boils, add **2 c. cous cous**—(or according to directions on package). Fluff it in with a fork. Turn off stove and let stand 5 minutes.

After standing, fluff again with fork. Cool.

Add:
3/4 c. green pepper, chopped fine
2 c. cucumber, cut in cubes
4 med. tomatoes, firm, chopped in small pieces
2 t. peppermint leaves
(rub between palms of hands to make fine)

3/4 c. olives, black, pitted and sliced
2 T. pimento, canned, cut fine
1 t. onion salt
1/2 t. salt

Emulsify in a small bottle:

4 T. lemon juice, fresh
3 T. oil
1/4 t. salt

Add to salad and mix well. (May make in the morning and serve at noon.)

Note: To reconstitute bulgar wheat to use in place of cous cous.
In pot: **4 c. water, boiling**
Add: **2 c. bulgar wheat (see p. 1)**
1/2 t. salt

TOFU COTTAGE CHEESE

In bowl:

2-1/4 c. tofu, crumbled firm (about 2 cubes)
1/2 t. garlic salt
1/2 t. onion salt
1/3 c. Soy Mayonnaise (see p. 83)

Mix well and serve.
Optional: Just add 1/2 t. salt instead of garlic and onion salt. Serve with peach halves and avacado or pears and avacado.

PINEAPPLE TOFU COTTAGE CHEESE

Add to Tofu Cottage Cheese (see p. 78):

drained pineapple chunks, cut in smaller pieces

Serve on frilly lettuce leaf.

or as individual salad—frilly lettuce leaf and 1 scoop Tofu Cottage Cheese on slice of pineapple

TOFU COTTAGE CHEESE FOR FESTIVE OCCASIONS (Individual Salads)

For Vegetable Meal
In bowl:

2 c. tofu, crumbled firm (about 2 cubes)

Add: **3 *or* 4 green onions, chopped**
2 T. parsley, chopped or snipped with scissors
1/2 t. garlic salt
1/2 t. onion salt
2 T. olives, black, pitted and sliced
1/3 c. to 1/2 c. Soy Mayonnaise (see p. 83)
salt to taste, if needed

Optional: 1/2 stalk celery, chopped fine instead of parsley. Serve a scoop on a leaf of lettuce with a dash of paprika on top. Garnish with radish rose.

continued...

For Fruit Meal

2 c.	**tofu, crumbled**
1/4 c.	**green pepper, chopped fine**
1/4 c.	**red pepper, chopped fine**
2 T.	**olives, black, pitted and sliced**
a little	**cucumber, chopped in small cuts**
1/2 t.	**garlic salt**
1/2 t.	**onion salt**
	salt to taste, if needed
1/3 c. to 1/2 c.	**Soy Mayonnaise (see p. 83)**

Slice 3 green pepper rings very fine.
Put a scoop of this "Festive" Tofu Cottage Cheese on top.
Garnish with 1 black olive or red bell pepper on top.

TOSSED SALAD

In large bowl:

lettuce pieces
spinach pieces
a little purple cabbage, shredded (for color)
or **purple onion slices, cut in 1/2 slices**
salt lightly, to taste

LEMON JUICE DRESSING

For large salad:

1/4 c.	**lemon juice**
1/4 c.	**oil**
1/8 t.	**salt**

Shake in small bottle.
For small salad—1/2 of dressing recipe.
Optional: Add 1/4 t. dill weed to above dressing *or* garlic powder *or* fresh, crushed garlic

WALDORF SALAD

Mix together in bowl:

3 *or* **4**	**red apples, washed, cored and diced** (do not peel)
1/2 c.	**dates, chopped**
1/2 c.	**walnuts, chopped**

Moisten with Soy Mayonnaise (see p. 83). Garnish with apple wedges and green pepper slices. Prepare just before serving.

"GROWING SPROUTS"

Best seeds to sprout:

lentils, soybeans, sunflower, alfalfa, rye, oats, wheat

1/2 c. seed = 1 c. soaked = 1 quart sprouts
fine seeds (i.e. alfalfa) 3 T. = 1 quart sprouts

1. Select good quality seeds.
2. Wash well.
3. Soak overnight in twice as much lukewarm water as seeds.

Bottle Method

Use a 1 or 2 quart jar with large mouth.
Cover jar with cheese cloth or fine mesh or fine screen over the mouth of the jar. Screw jar ring in place.

Measure seeds. Wash.
Soak overnight.
Drain in the morning, turning jar upside down to drain well. Gently shake seeds to distribute evenly on sides of jar. First day (or 2 for alfalfa sprouts)—wrap in warm towel and put on counter. Turn bottle on side.

Rinse with warm water morning and evening.
Drain well and place on side after rinsing.
Note: For sprouts that take longer to sprout, cover and keep warm at least 1 day. Then uncover and place in sunlight for nice green sprouts, always remembering to turn jar on side.

Seeds	Amount	Sprouting	Best Length
Dry lentil	3/4 cup	3–4 days	1/2 inch
Sunflower	1 cup	2 days	1/4 inch
Garbanzo (chick peas)	1 cup	3 days	1 inch
Alfalfa	3 Tbsp.	4–5 days	1–2 inches
Soybean	1 cup	3 days	1/2–3/4 inch
Whole wheat	1 cup	5 days	1-1/2–2 inches

When sprouts have reached harvest length, put in covered container and refrigerate.
Use over next 3 or 4 days for optimum nutrition.

WHY SPROUT?

1. Fewer calories with less carbohydrates.
2. An increase of riboflavin and vitamin "C".
3. Green sprouts—vitamin "A".
4. Use in salads, sandwiches, Chinese recipes, stir frys, and patties.

LEMON JUICE VS. VINEGAR

Bronson, in "Nutrition and Food Chemistry", declares that vinegar lengthens the time that vegetables remain in the stomach. Vinegar's acidity hinders digestion.

"Vinegar is naturally or artificially flavored acetic acid, commonly ranging between 4 and 6 percent.... Mild gastritis or enteritis may be caused by it." —Journal of the American Medical Association.

Lemon juice is a delightful substitute.

"PICKLED" BEETS WITH LEMONADE

Boil beets until tender and peel.
Slice or dice to desired size. Salt to taste.
Cover with undiluted, frozen lemonade (thawed) and let stand for 24 hours.

Drain and serve as pickled beets.

CREAMY DRESSING FOR CUCUMBERS

Blend in blender till creamy:

1/3 rounded c. cashews, raw, washed
1/3 c. cucumber pieces
1/4 t. onion salt
1 T. lemon juice, fresh (if you like it more "lemony", add 1 more t. lemon juice)
1 T. honey, liquid (light)
1/4 t. garlic salt

Put in jar and store in refrigerator till ready to use.

COLE SLAW DRESSING

Mix well:

- **1/2 c. Soy Mayonnaise** **(see p. 83)**
- **1 T. pineapple juice,** or to desired consistency
- **1 t. honey, liquid**

KETCHUP

Blend until smooth and refrigerate:

- **1–5.5 oz. can "Hunts" tomato paste + water** (fill can 1/4 full and rinse, adding to above)
- **1 T. honey, liquid**
- **1/4 t. salt**
- **1/4 t. onion powder**
- **1/4 t. garlic powder**
- **1 T. oil**
- **1 T. lemon juice**
- **pinch of oregano**

MOCK MUSTARD

Blend in blender:

- **1 c. "Real Lemon" juice, bottled**
- **1/4 c. flour, unbleached white**

Put above in small pot and cook until thickened, stirring constantly. Cool.

Blend in blender 1 minute:

- **1/3 c. cashews**
- **1/3 c. water**

Add the above thickened lemon juice to the creamy cashews and blend .

Add:

- **1/2 t. onion salt**
- **1/3 c. oil**
- **2 cloves garlic**
- **1/2 t. tumeric**
- **2 T. honey, liquid**

Put in glass container and keep in the refrigerator. Will keep about 1 week.

LEMON HERB DRESSING

Shake in small bottle to mix, with lid on:

4 T. oil
3 T. lemon juice
1/8 t. garlic salt
1/8 t. onion salt

Keep in refrigerator till ready to use.
Note: Add fresh dill to salads or garlic or herbs of choice for special flavors!

SESAME SALAD DRESSING

Shake ingredients in small bottle to mix:

1/4 c. oil, chilled
1/4 c. lemon juice, fresh
1/4 t. onion salt

Use desired amount on salad and refrigerate what is not used. Sprinkle over salad **3 T. toasted sesame seeds.**
Note: Toast unhulled sesame seeds in 300° F. oven for 10 minutes. Toast extra to have on hand for salads and cereals!

SOY MAYONNAISE

Blend in blender till creamy:

1 c. water
2/3 c. "Loma Linda Soyagen" powder
(with no cane or beet sugar)
1/4 t. garlic powder
1/4 t. celery salt
3/4 t. onion salt

Add chilled corn oil while blending till mayonnaise is thick. Put in bowl.

Add: **2 T. + 2 t. lemon juice, fresh**

Mix well. Put in jar and refrigerate.

SOY "NUT OR SEED" MAYONNAISE

Blend in blender till creamy:

1 c. **water**
1/2 c. **"Loma Linda Soyagen" powder**
1/4 t. **garlic salt**
1/4 t. **celery salt**
1/2 t. **onion salt**
1/2 c. **cashews, raw, washed**
or **1/2 c.sunflower seeds**
or **1/2 c. pumpkin seeds**

Continue blending till thick. Put in bowl.
Add 2 T. + 2 t. fresh lemon juice.
Mix well. Put in jar and refrigerate.

TARTAR SAUCE

In bowl:

1 c. **Soy Mayonnaise (see p. 83)**
1 T. **green onion, chopped**
2 T. **olives, chopped**
or **a little fresh dill**
2 T. **celery, chopped**

Mix and serve.

THOUSAND ISLAND DRESSING

Mix well in bowl:

2 c. **Soy Mayonnaise (see p. 83)**
1/4 t. **dill weed or to taste**
1/4 c. **celery, chopped very fine**
3 *or* **4** **green onions, chopped very fine**
1 T. **homemade Ketchup (see p. 82) or to taste**

Pour into container. Refrigerate.

TOFU MAYONNAISE (OR DIP!)

Blend till creamy in blender:

1/2 c. cashews
1/2 c. water

Add and blend:

1 c. tofu, crumbled
1/2 t. celery salt
3/4 t. onion salt
1/8 t. garlic salt
2 t. Mock Chicken Seasoning #1 (see p. 119)
1 T. lemon juice, fresh
1/4 c. more water to blend
dill to taste

Put in jar and refrigerate.

AVOCADO MAYONNAISE (OR DIP!)

Mash 1 avocado and add equal amount of Tofu Mayonnaise (see p. 85). Add salt to taste.

TOFU SOUR CREAM

Blend in blender till creamy, 1 minute:

3 T. cashews
1/4 c. water

Add and blend again:

1 c. more water
1 c. tofu, firm, drained and crumbled (about 1 cube)
1/2 t. salt
1/4 t. onion salt
2 t. lemon juice
1/8 t. dill seed *or* **fresh dill**

Put in bowl and add:

2 *or* **3 slices green onions**

Optional: Instead of dill, add:

1 clove garlic, minced
1 T. parsley.

TOMATO FRENCH DRESSING

Blend in blender:

2/3 c. tomato juice
1/4 c. "Hunts" tomato paste

Add the following items one at a time as blender is blending:

2 t. dried onion, minced
pinch of oregano
1/4 t. garlic salt
1/3 c. corn oil
3 T. lemon juice, fresh
1/4 t. salt
1 T. honey, liquid
1/4 c. water

Blend till creamy. Pour in jar. Store in refrigerator till ready to use. Nicest when freshly made.

TOMATO FRENCH DRESSING (ORIGINAL RECIPE)

Blend in blender till creamy:

1–10 oz. can tomato soup
1/3 c. corn oil
1 t. dried onion, minced
3 T. lemon juice, fresh
1/2 t. salt
1 T. honey, liquid

Put in bottle. Keep in refrigerator.

Health is a blessing of which few appreciate the value; yet upon it the efficiency of our mental and physical powers largely depend. Christ's Object Lessons, p. 346.

Thought for the day

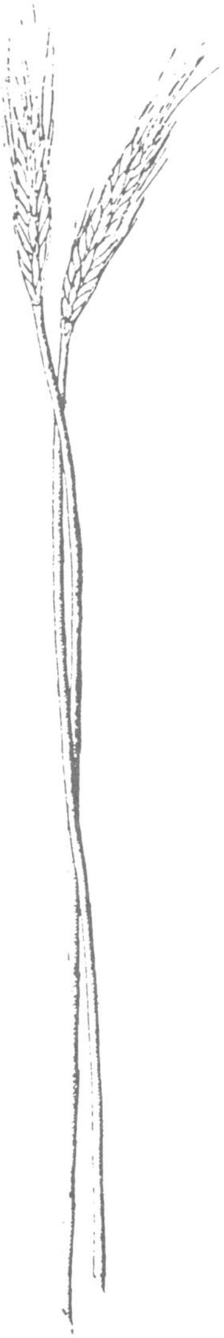

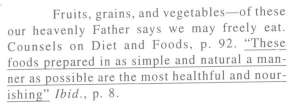

Fruits, grains, and vegetables—of these our heavenly Father says we may freely eat. Counsels on Diet and Foods, p. 92. "These foods prepared in as simple and natural a manner as possible are the most healthful and nourishing" *Ibid.*, p. 8.

A simple salad, sliced tomatoes, fresh fruits and vegetables—these are easy to prepare and they are good for us. "The more we depend upon the fresh fruit just as it is plucked from the tree, the greater will be the blessing." *Ibid.*, p.309.

A beautiful lesson is shared in Luke 10:38-42 NIV.

As Jesus and his disciples were on their way, he came to a village where a woman named Martha opened her home to him. She had a sister called Mary, who sat at the Lord's feet listening to what He said. But Martha was distracted by all the preparations that had to be made. She came to him and asked, "Lord, don't you care that my sister has left me to do the work by myself? Tell her to help me!" "Martha, Martha", the Lord answered, "you are worried and upset about many things, but only one thing is needed. Mary has chosen what is better, and it will not be taken from her."

Mary's devotion was heart appreciation for Jesus and His great mission of love. Oh, that we might understand the truth about the cross and His great love for us.

Remember, God loves you.

Notes

Vegetables & Fruit Dishes

VEGETABLES

1. Vegetables should be used as soon as possible after harvesting.
2. Thoroughly wash before using. Store in refrigerator if necessary.
3. Avoid soaking.
4. Cook vegetables whole or in large pieces for maximum nutrition.
5. Use as little water as possible or steam vegetables.
6. Start vegetables in boiling water; add vegetables; bring to boil again; then lower the heat.
7. Cook as short a time as possible, just before eating. Serve immediately.
8. Save any liquid for soups, gravies, etc.
9. Season and salt lastly and lightly.

Include a dark green or yellow vegetable in the menu every day for vitamin "A". Vegetables, as listed below, are also high in calcium—such as: Beet Greens, Broccoli, Carrots, Kale, Sweet Potatoes, Squash and Parsley.

Eat plenty of greens to replace nutrients formerly provided by the milk group... "on a weight basis, mixed green leafy vegetables supply as much calcium and riboflavin as milk."

"(Where calcium is concerned, spinach and chard are exceptions to this rule. They contain a compound called oxalic acid, which combines with calcium to make it largely unabsorbable to the body.)" Dr. Kenneth Burke.

Whether therefore ye eat, or drink, or whatsoever ye do, do all to the glory of God. I Corinthians 10:31.

The little attentions, the small acts of love and self-sacrifice, that flow from the life as quietly as the fragrance from a flower—these constitute no small share of the blessings and happiness of life. The Faith I Live By, p. 267.

CALCIUM IN COMMON FOODS

FOOD SOURCE		CAL	PRO *gm*	CHO *gm*	FAT *gm*	Na *mg*	Ca *mg*
Human breast milk	1 c.	184	2.4	22.4	9.6	40	80
Cow's milk:							
whole, fresh	1 c.	159	8.5	12.0	8.6	122	288
nonfat, skim	1 c.	88	8.8	12.6	.2	128	298
nonfat, skim, fort.	1 c.	105	9.8	13.9	1.2	142	359
Soy milk:							
"Loma Linda Soyagen", all-purpose	1 c.	146	7.3	11.0	8.5	303	72
Broccoli, cooked	1 c.	32	4.1	6.0	.4	13	117
Collards, cooked	1 c.	58	5.4	9.8	1.2	50	304
Lambsquarters,cooked	1 c.	64	6.4	10.0	1.4		516
Mustard greens,cooked	1 c.	46	4.4	8.0	.8	36	276
Sesame seeds, whole	2 T.	125	4.1	4.8	10.9	13	258
Sunflower seed kernel	2 T.	124	5.3	4.4	10.5	6.7	27
Soybeans, cooked	1 c.	260	22.0	21.6	11.4	4	146
Kale, cooked	1 c.	48	5.3	7.5	1.0	94	224
Oatmeal cereal, cooked	1 c.	123	56.0	23.3	.8	169	191
Cream of wheat, cooked	1 c.	130	4.4	26.9	.4	96	185

ASPARAGUS ON TOAST

Make **1 recipe Savory Cream Sauce** (see p. 68).
Serve on individual plates:

1 slice toast
desired amount of Savory Cream Sauce
cooked asparagus spears on top

HARVARD BEETS

Dice cooked beets.
Season with a little salt.
Add undiluted frozen lemonade to taste.
Thicken with a little arrowroot or cornstarch.

CABBAGE ROLLS I

Wash and core cabbage. Put whole cabbage in a big pot of hot water at boiling point. Steam off leaves one at a time, separating them with a fork and knife. Steam each leaf approximately one minute or till just pliable (don't overcook or it will tear). Gently remove each steamed leaf to a big bowl to cool.

FILLING

Sauté in 1 T. oil:

	2 med.	**onions, chopped fine**
or	**1 lg.**	**onion**
	2/3 c.	**celery, chopped fine**
	1 c.	**tofu, frozen, thawed then shredded**

Season with:

	1 t.	**Maggi (see p. 2)**
	2 t.	**Bisto (see p. 1)**

Put above ingredients in bowl.

Add:	**2-1/2 c.**	**brown rice, cooked and lightly-salted**
	1 T.	**Bisto (see p. 1)**
	1/2 t.	**onion salt**
	1/2 c.	**walnuts, ground**
	1/2 t.	**garlic salt**

Mix well. Put in center of each cabbage leaf 1 heaping tablespoon of the above mixture. Roll in cabbage leaf and tuck in. Put in casserole.

BROTH TO POUR OVER CABBAGE ROLLS

Sauté in 1 t. oil and a little water, if necessary:

	1 sm.	**onion, chopped fine**
Add:	**1 c**	**water**
	2 t.	**Bisto (see p. 1)**
	1/2 t.	**onion salt**

Simmer just 1 minute.
Pour broth over cabbage rolls and cover the casserole.
Bake at 350° F. for 1/2 to 1 hour, just till the cabbage is tender.

Note: My daughter-in-law likes to double the broth recipe on her cabbage rolls, you might, too!

CABBAGE ROLLS II

Grandchildren's Favorite

Prepare cabbage leaves by same method as Cabbage Rolls I (see p. 92).

FILLING

Sauté in 1 T. oil:

1 lg. **onion, chopped fine**
1 clove **garlic, chopped very fine**

Put above in big bowl.

Add: **2-1/2 c.** **brown rice, cooked**

Sauté in Silverstone frying pan:

2 c. **tofu, frozen, thawed, sliced and cut in small cubes**
2 T. **Mock Chicken Seasoning #2 (see p. 119)**
2 t. **Maggi (see p. 2)**
2 t. **Bisto (see p. 1)**

Add seasoned tofu to bowl with rice.

Add: **1 T.** **Bisto (see p. 1)**
1/2 t. **onion salt**
1/2 t. **garlic salt**

Mix well. Put in center of each cabbage leaf 1 heaping tablespoon of above mixture. Roll in cabbage leaf and tuck in. Put in casserole.

Pour broth over cabbage rolls and cover.
Bake at 350° F. for 1/2 to 1 hour or till the cabbage is tender.

Thanks Mary Lutyk and Gizella Lawson for helping with this recipe!

Christ fought the battle upon the point of appetite, and came off victorious; and we also can conquer through strength derived from him. ... Christ has resisted the power of him who would hold us in bondage; ... He withstood temptation, and proved by this act that our cases are not hopeless. ... We have a living Saviour, who is ready and willing to aid us! ... to everyone who will unite his weak, wavering will to the omnipotent, unwavering will of God. Counsels on Diet and Foods, *p. 169, 170*

BROCCOLI RICE SUPREME

Cook **1 c. brown rice** according to directions.
Cook **1 c. white basmati rice** according to directions.

Sauté in 1 t. oil and 2 T. water, till still crunchy:

1 lg.	**onion**
1 stalk	**celery, chopped fine**

Mix both rices together lightly and fluff.

Add:		**sautéed onion and celery**
	2 t.	**Mock Chicken Seasoning #2 (see p. 119)**

Mix well.
Put the above mixture in a fairly shallow Pyrex dish.
Pour over the rice:

	1-1/2 c.	**Cashew Pimento Cheese Sauce (see p. 65)**
or		**Mockzarella Cheese Sauce (see p. 67)**

Steam desired amount of broccoli flowerettes.
Season with **1/4 t. salt**.
Arrange broccoli flowerettes attractively on rice.
Add a trickle of Cashew Pimento Cheese or Mockzarella Cheese Sauce on stems only.

Optional: Garnish with black, pitted olive slices.

CONFETTI RICE

Season rice to taste with Rhona Clarke's Irish Curry (see p. 120) or Mock Chicken Seasoning #2 (see p. 119).

Just before serving, add 1/4 c. mixed vegetables, barely cooked. Toss in just enough for a medley of color through rice.

HERBED CARROTS

12–16 sm.	**carrots, tender, cooked**
1/4 t.	**marjoram**
1/8 t.	**basil**

Salt lightly to taste.
Sprinkle chopped parsley on sparingly.

CREAMED CARROTS AND POTATOES

Boil small potatoes and salt lightly.
Cook separately—2" carrot sticks.
Combine the above.
Add just a little Savory Sauce
Just before serving, sprinkle with chopped parsley
or add frozen green peas for color.

CAULIFLOWER OR BROCCOLI
WITH CASHEW PIMENTO CHEESE SAUCE

Cook cauliflower flowerettes or broccoli spears till almost done.
Salt lightly and drain.
Just before serving, cover with Cashew Pimento Cheese Sauce (see p. 65).

LAYERED CAULIFLOWER

Barely cook cauliflower in generous size flowerettes.

Make: **1 recipe Tofu Mayonnaise (see p. 85)**
1 c. bread crumbs, toasted (or more if desired)

Use an approximately 7" x 7" x 3" deep casserole dish.
Grease casserole and sprinkle toasted whole wheat bread crumbs on the bottom of the casserole. Add a layer of cauliflower flowerettes. Pour over the cauliflower, 1/2 of the Tofu Mayonnaise. Sprinkle whole wheat bread crumbs.

Repeat—cauliflower, then Tofu Mayonnaise and top with crumbs. Heat in oven at 350° F. for 30 minutes.

GREEN BEANS WITH SLICED ALMONDS

Steam green beans until tender.
Place in serving dish and sprinkle with salt to taste.
Sprinkle toasted, sliced almonds on top.

CORN SOUFFLÉ

Cook in a small amount of water:

2-1/2 c. corn, frozen

Add: **1/4 t. salt**

Drain well. (May use fresh cooked corn, cut off the cob, adding 1/4 t. salt.)

Place cooked corn in bowl.

Add: **1/2 c. soymilk**
1 c. tofu, crumbled (about 1 cube)
1/4 t. salt
1/4 t. garlic salt
1/4 t. onion salt
3 T. cornmeal (dry grain)

Mix well. Pour in greased casserole.
Bake one hour at 350° F.
(Best eaten the same day and not reheated.)

SPANISH EGGPLANT WITH KIDNEY BEANS

Sauté in saucepan in 1 T. oil:

1 green pepper, washed and chopped fine

Add: **4 c. tomatoes, canned**
1/8 t. oregano
1/2 t. celery salt
1/4 t. onion salt
3/4 t. sweet basil
1/2 t. garlic salt
1 t. honey, liquid (if tomatoes are tart—add honey to taste)
2 T. Engevita yeast **(see p. 2)**

Add: **1 lg. eggplant, cubed** (wash and leave skin on)

Cook till just done, about 5 minutes.

Add: **1–2 cups kidney beans, drained, cooked,** salted lightly while cooking

Thicken with cornstarch or arrowroot to desired consistency. Place in a casserole.

Serve over fluffy brown rice.

STUFFED GREEN PEPPERS

Bring to boil:

5 c. water
2 t. salt

Add and simmer until cooked (about 20 minutes):

2 c. white rice, "Uncle Ben's" converted

or **1 c. brown rice, cooked and**
1 c. white rice, cooked

Add to rice and mix:

1 recipe Cashew Pimento Cheese Sauce (see p. 65)
adding **1 T. Engevita yeast (see p. 2) and**
1 t. onion powder
1 piece pimento, canned, chopped
2 c. garbanzos (chick peas), drained (1–19 oz. can)

Steam for 10 minutes:

5–6 med. green bell peppers

Fill peppers with rice filling and bake in Pyrex dish for 30 minutes at 375° F. Before serving, sprinkle with paprika.

or

RICE CASSEROLE—Place rice filling in casserole and bake 30 minutes at 375° F.

Optional: Mix in 1/2 c. sautéed green bell peppers.

Exercise and a free and abundant use of the air and sunlight are blessings which Heaven has freely bestowed upon all. Counsels on Health, p. 54.

MILLET STUFFED PEPPERS

In saucepan, bring to boil:

	2 c.	**tomato juice**
	1/2 c.	**water**
	1-1/2 t.	**Mock Chicken Seasoning #2 (see p. 119)**
Add:	**1 c.**	**millet, hulled**

Bring to boil, then simmer 35 minutes.
Fold in:

1 c.	**Cashew Pimento Cheese (see p. 65)** (or 1-1/4 c. if you want them more moist)

Stuff in 4 large green peppers or 6 medium or 8 small.
Put in a baking dish that can be covered.

Add:	**2 c.**	**water**
seasoned with:	**2 T.**	**Mock Chicken Seasoning #2**

Steam for 1 hour at 350° F. If large, peppers may be cut in half when served.

STUFFED BAKED POTATOES

Select well-shaped potatoes of about equal size.
Wash, prick and bake until soft. Cut top off of potato lengthwise.
Scoop baked potato in bowl.

Add soymilk and salt to taste. Mash till fluffy.
Fill the potato skins with mashed potato, swirling up on top.
Reheat in Pyrex dish till heated through.

Optional: Put a sprinkle of paprika on top
or a dab of Mockzarella Cheese Sauce (see p. 67)and sprinkle of paprika.

CHEEZY POTATOES

A suggestion to try.
Steam small potatoes or potato chunks. Salt lightly.
Just before serving, pour over potatoes Mockzarella Cheese Sauce (see p. 67).
Sprinkle with chopped chives or parsley, as desired.

HASH BROWN POTATO PANCAKES

Boil 4 medium potatoes with skins on. Cool.
Peel potatoes.
In large bowl—dice potatoes fine.
Mix together, then add to potatoes:

3 T. flour
1/4 c. soymilk
1/2 t. garlic powder
1-1/2 t. onion powder
salt to taste

Mix well.
Spoon on lightly oiled Silverstone frying pan in pancake shapes. When "hash" potato pancake is golden, turn over. Delicious with Scrambled Tofu (see p. 143) for a hearty breakfast.

Thanks Bea Sohm for sharing your recipe!

OVEN FRIES

Scrub potatoes and peel. Slice lengthwise 2" or 3" long, 1/4" wide as chips. Place on lightly oiled Silverstone cookie sheet with 1 T. oil or less.

Bake at 375 degrees for 1/2 hour or till done. Salt lightly.
Note: Length of time depends on how full your cookie sheet is and size of potatoes, etc.

NEW POTATOES WITH CHIVES

Steam new potatoes with skins. Remove skins. If small, leave whole or cut to desired size.

Add: finely chopped chives for color and flavor, as desired. Salt lightly.

Optional: In place of chives, parsley snipped with scissors.

HAZELNUT "PATTYCAKES"—FOR MOM

"Pattycakes"—For Mom

For leftover mashed potatoes.
In small pot:

2 c.	**water, cold**
1/2 c.	**cornmeal**
1/4 t.	**salt**

Bring to boil, stirring occasionally. Lower heat to simmer for 15 minutes.

Sauté in 1 t. oil and 1 T. water:

1 med.- lg.	**onion, chopped fine**
1/4 t.	**salt**

Put both of above in bowl.

Add:	**1/4 t.**	**celery salt**
	2/3 c.	**hazel nuts, coarsley ground**
	1/2 t.	**sage**
	1/4 t.	**onion salt**
	2 c.	**mashed potatoes, lightly-salted**

Form in patties. Fry on Silverstone frying pan with a trickle of oil till golden on each side.

SCALLOPED POTATOES

Blend in blender until creamy (1 minute):

1 c.	**cashews, raw**
1 c.	**water**

Add and blend:

2 t.	**Mock Chicken Seasoning #1 (see p. 119)**
2 t.	**salt or to taste**
1 T. + 1 t.	**arrowroot powder**
1-1/2 c.	**water**

Add:	**1-1/2 c.**	**water**

Wash, peel and thinly slice:

8 med.-lg.	**potatoes**
1	**onion, chopped fine**

continued...

In casserole combine alternately, layers of milk mixture, potatoes and onions—beginning and ending with milk mixture. Cover with lid or foil. Bake at 400° F. for 30 minutes. Remove cover and bake at 375° F. for 1 hour and 20 minutes or until done.

BAKED SWEET POTATOES

Try to choose same size so they will be done at the same time or cut to size.

Wash potatoes well.
Bake at 375° F. for approximately 60 minutes.

A Quicker Way—Place in a casserole with a little water on the bottom. Cover and let steam till just done. Remove from casserole and allow to finish baking on rack in oven.

To serve, cut in halves, peel and serve with Pineapple Sauce.

PINEAPPLE SAUCE—pineapple juice (sweetened, if desired) thickened with cornstarch or arrowroot
or mash, and season with salt to taste and

Add: **2 T. pineapple, drained and crushed per sweet potato**, depending on size or desired amounts.

Optional: **1** or **2 T. coconut, unsweetenedand shredded**

or scoop (ice cream scoop) mashed sweet potato on slice of pineapple and serve.

BAKED ACORN SQUASH

Bake till done in 375° F. oven.
Slice in half lengthwise and scoop out seeds.
Salt lightly and place in desired size of Pyrex dish.
Pour in center of squash:

1 t. maple syrup
Add: **1 T. raisins, washed**

Reheat and serve.

ORANGE HONEY ACORN SQUASH

Wash acorn squash. Put in flat pan to bake whole.
Prick 2 vents with sharp knife in each squash.
Bake at 350° F. for 1 hour or till just barely done (time depends on size of squash).

GLAZE
Slice squash in half and scoop out seeds.
Put squash back on flat pan.
For each acorn squash (2 halves), mix together:

- **1 T. orange juice, frozen, thawed and unsweetened**
- **1 t. honey, liquid**

Pour into center of squash.
Make enough glaze for number of squash being baked.
Put back in oven and bake 10–15 minutes.

SPAGHETTI SQUASH AND SAUCE

Cut spaghetti squash lengthwise and remove seeds. Bake cut-side down 45 mins. at 350° F. Turn over and bake until skin is tender. Serve fluffed up like spaghetti on each plate.

SAUCE (to serve on spaghetti squash)

Blend in blender:

- **2 apples, cored**
- **2 pears, peeled and cored**
- enough water to blend smoothly

Place above in saucepan.

Add:
- **12 med. tomatoes, peeled and cut up**
- **2 apples, cored and cut up small**
- **2 pears, cored and cut up small**
- **1/2 t. garlic powder**
- **1 t. honey, liquid**
- **1 t. sweet basil**
- **1/2 t. salt or to taste**
- **3 oz. tomato paste or to taste**
- **1/2 green pepper, cut fine**

Slow simmer for 45 minutes to 1 hr. till well-blended.

Thanks Olive Lowe for sharing recipe!

VEGETABLES WITH CREAM SAUCE AND CURRY — "A Favorite"

In pot:

4 c. **potatoes, cubed**
1 med. **onion, chopped fine**
1-1/2 c. **water**
1/2 t. **salt**

Cook till barely done.
Cook separately:

2 *or* **3** **carrots, cut in 1" strips**
1/2 c. **water**
1/8 t. **salt**

Drain before adding to other vegetables.
Cook till just done:

1–12 oz. pkg. **Fordhook green lima beans, frozen (350 g.)**

Drain any broth for soups.
Combine all vegetables in large pot and add:

1/4 t. **garlic salt**
1/4 t. **celery salt**
1/4 t. **onion salt**

Blend in blender 1 minute:

1 c. **cashews, raw**
1 c. **water**
salt to taste, if needed
3 t. **arrowroot powder**
3 *or* **4 t.** **Rhona Clarke's Irish Curry (see p. 120)**

Heat sauce, add vegetables and serve immediately.
Serve on fluffy rice.

Beloved, I wish above all things that thou mayest prosper and be in health, even as thy soul prospereth. John III, v. 2.

SUCCOTASH

Cook till done:

2 c. corn, frozen
1/4 c. water
1/4 t. salt

Cook till done:

1 c. green limas, frozen
1/4 c. water
1/8 t. salt

Combine corn and frozen green limas and serve.
Optional: Finely chopped green or red bell pepper or both. Sauté lightly, so still bright with color. Add to succotash and toss lightly.

VEGETABLE POT PIE—"A Favorite"

Boil in small amount of water till barely done:

6 med. potatoes, diced in 1/2" cubes, lightly-salted

Drain when done and save potato water.
In separate pot, cook till barely done:

4 *or* 5 med. carrots, sliced or cut

In separate pot, cook in small amount of water:

1–12 oz. pkg. Fordhook green limas, frozen
salt to taste

Sauté in 1 t. oil and 3 T. water:

1 med. onion, chopped fine
2 stalks celery, chopped fine
1/4 t. salt

Drain above vegetables and save liquid for soup.
Combine all the above vegetables in a large bowl.

Make: **1 recipe Savory Cream Sauce (see p. 68).**

Add: **1/2 c. potato water, drained off potatoes**
1/4 t. garlic salt
salt to taste

continued...

Mix all together gently. Pour into Pyrex dish. Cover with favorite pastry and prick or cut a design.

Bake at 400° F. for 35–45 minutes or till crust is done and golden.

Note: Try Brown Gravy instead of Savory Cream Sauce for a change.
or serve as a stew without pastry
or creamed vegetables on fluffy brown rice

"WINTER GARDEN" STIR-FRY

Prepare vegetables first—keeping sections together:

A) **1 lg. onion, chopped fine**
2–3 cloves garlic, minced

B) **7 med. carrots, (6") peeled and cut diagonally 1" to 1-1/2"**
4 parsnips, peeled and cut diagonally 1" to 1-1/2"

C) **3 lg. leeks** (and green tops sliced—if nice)
3 stalks celery, cut diagonally
1 c. broccoli flowerettes

Preheat electric frying pan—325 to 350° F. Sauté 3 minutes in 1 T. oil:

(A) **onion and garlic**
1/4 c. water

Add:

(B) **carrots and parsnips**
1/3 c. water

Cover with lid—about 5 minutes—don't let it go dry.

Add:

(C) **leeks, celery and broccoli**

Add water as needed—1/2 c. at a time. Let steam until barely tender. Season lightly with salt and:

1 t. Maggi (see p. 2)

Serve immediately with fluffy rice and a Tossed Salad (see p. 79).

Thanks Donna Hastings for sharing a recipe!

STUFFED ZUCCHINI (Makes 8)

2–7" zucchinis—cut lengthwise in half and cut again in the middle (makes 4 quarters for each zucchini)

Steam sections until almost cooked. Scoop out fleshy part and seeds—set aside.

Lightly salt each little section and place in Pyrex dish. Cook filling:

1 c. tomato juice
1 c. Walnut Wheat Crumbles (see p. 38)
1/2 t. Bisto (see p. 1)
1/8 t. garlic salt
1/2 t. sweet basil

Simmer until mixture is thick and rehydrated.

Add: **1 c. brown rice, cooked**
1 T. Cashew Pimento Cheese (see p. 65)
scooped-out zucchini, chopped

Fill the zucchini boats with filling and sprinkle toasted whole wheat bread crumbs on top and reheat in oven at 325° F. until heated. It's delicious!

TASTY ZUCCHINI

Wash zucchini well—don't peel.
Grate zucchini.
Steam or cook until barely done.
Salt lightly.
At the table—sprinkle generously with Engevita yeast (see p. 2) and a dash of onion salt.

The home should be to the children the most attractive place in the world and the mother's presence should be its greatest attraction. By gentle discipline, in loving words and acts, mothers may bind the children to their hearts. The Faith I Live By, p. 264.

Thought for the day

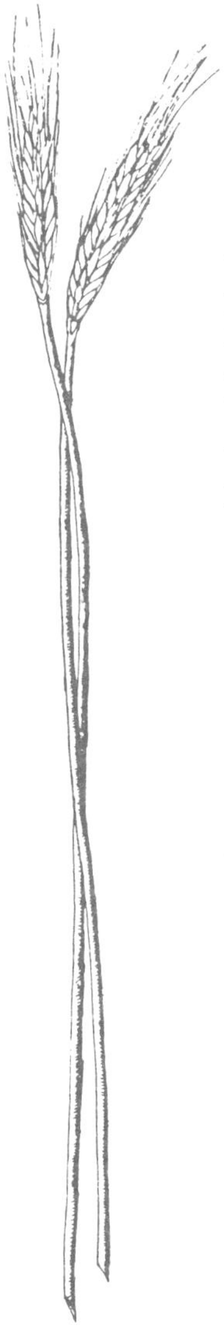

"Better a meal of vegetables
where there is love
than a fattened calf with hatred."

Proverbs 15:17 NIV.

"Love is patient, love is kind. It does not envy, it does not boast, it is not proud. It is not rude, it is not self-seeking, it is not easily angered, it keeps no record of wrongs. Love does not delight in evil but rejoices with the truth. It always protects, always trusts, always hopes, always perseveres. Love never fails."
I Corinthians 13:4-8 first part NIV.

What a joy to share a meal with someone who has true love—one who loves you even though you have been selfish, unkind, or insulting, who forgives and sees only what you may become by Christ's presence and grace. One who loves from a purely unselfish motive, because He loves you.

That's the kind of love God has for us. The gift of Christ is for everyone. Like the sunshine, each one gets all the light that shines as if he is the only person in all the world.

When Jesus lives in our hearts by faith He brings His faith and love into our lives.

Isn't it good news to know He "loved me and gave Himself for me"? Galatians 2:20 last part.

Remember, God loves you.

Soups

"CHICK" NOODLE SOUP

In large pot:

2 med.	**potatoes, washed, peeled and grated** (about 1-1/2 c.)
1 stalk	**celery, chopped very fine**
1 sm.	**onion, chopped very fine**
1/4 t.	**salt**
3 c.	**water**
1	**bay leaf**

Bring to boil and simmer 20 minutes.

Add:	**4 c.**	**water**
	1–19 oz. can	**garbanzos (chick peas) and liquid**
	1 med.	**carrot, grated**

Bring to boil again

Add: **1 sm. handful** **thin soy noodles, broken**

Boil gently for 15 minutes. Remove bay leaf.

Add:	**1 T.**	**Mock Chicken Seasoning #2 (see p. 119)**
	1/2 t.	**celery salt**
	1/4 t.	**onion salt**
	1/2 t.	**garlic salt**

Just before serving add

1/4 c. **parsley, fresh, chopped fine**

CREAMY LENTIL SOUP

Multiply recipe to suit family.
Blend in blender:

1-1/2 c.	**Seasoned Lentils (see p. 48), cooked and drained**
1-1/2 c.	**water**
1/4 t.	**garlic salt**
1 T.	**Mock Chicken Seasoning #2 (see p. 119)**
1/4 t.	**onion salt**
1 t.	**arrowroot powder** *or* **cornstarch**

Pour above mixture into a pot. Stir occasionally until it comes to a boil.

Remove from heat, leave lid on until ready to serve.

Optional: Add 1/2 c. soy noodles (cooked separately).
or add leftover vegetables and use as creamy base.

CORN CHOWDER

Simmer until cooked:

1 med. onion, chopped
4 med. potatoes, cubed
6 c. water, hot
1 t. salt

Mash cooked mixture with potato masher only enough to break into small pieces.

Add: **1/4 t. sweet basil**
1/4 t. celery salt
2 c. corn, cooked

Blend until creamy (1 minute) and add to above:

2/3 c. cashews, raw
3/4 c. water
1 T. Mock Chicken Seasoning #1 (see p. 119)

Heat and serve. Do not boil.

LEGUME SOUP

Clean, wash and soak overnight:

1/2 c. dried green split peas
1/2 c. dried yellow split peas
1/2 c. dried baby lima beans
1/2 c. pot (hulled) barley (don't use pearl barley)

In the morning, drain water off. Put in big pot and add 2 quarts of fresh water. Bring to boil and simmer 3–4 hours until almost done. If mixture gets too thick, add water.

Add: **1 lg. onion, chopped fine**
2 potatoes, grated
3 med.-lg. carrots, grated
1 c. celery, chopped fine, plus leaves of stalk chopped fine

Add desired amount of water for vegetables and simmer 45 minutes or till done. Stir occasionally.

Season with salt, celery salt, and garlic salt to taste.

Add **1/4 c. fresh parsley snipped with scissors** just before serving (or 2 T. dried parsley, crumbled).

CREAM OF POTATO SOUP

Wash, peel, and chop in small pieces:

6 med.-lg. potatoes

Put in large pot.

Add: **8 c. water**
1 med.-lg. onion, chopped fine

Cook until done on simmer (about 45 minutes).
Mash with potato masher to make the potato pieces even smaller.

Add: **1-3/4 t. salt**
1/4 t. celery salt
1/4 t. paprika
1 t. Mock Chicken Seasoning #2 **(see p. 119)**
1/4 c. parsley, fresh, chopped fine
or **2 T. dehydrated parsley flakes, crumbled**

Blend in blender until creamy to make Cashew Cream:

1 c. cashews, raw
1 c. water

Add to soup—stir and serve. Don't let soup come to a boil after adding Cashew Cream.

If using a soymilk or other non-dairy milk—add 6 cups water when cooking potatoes and add 2 cups rich soymilk just before serving instead of Cashew Cream.

CREAM OF BROCCOLI SOUP

Using the above recipe base, steam broccoli and cut up in desired size. After broccoli is barely cooked, add approximately 2 c. chopped broccoli.

CREAM OF CAULIFLOWER SOUP

Use cauliflower in place of broccoli. You may want to add a little more cauliflower.

BONNIE'S SPLIT PEA SOUP

In large pot, add:

2 quarts	**water**
2 c.	**split peas**
1 stalk	**celery, chopped fine**
1 lg.	**carrot, grated**
1/4 t.	**thyme, ground**
1	**bay leaf**
	salt to taste

Cook until done.

Thanks Bonnie Laing for sharing recipe!

ZUCCHINI SOUP — "a quickie"

In large pot:

3 c.	**tomatoes, canned**
5 c.	**water**
6–6"	**zucchini** (or equivalent), **grated**
1–19 oz. can	**garbanzos (chick peas) and liquid**

Bring to boil and simmer 30 minutes.

Add:	**1-1/2–2 c.**	**green beans, french style**
	1 c.	**brown rice, cooked**
or		**equivalent soy noodles**

Bring to boil and simmer 20 minutes.
Season:

3/4 t.	**garlic salt**
1/4 t.	**celery salt**
1/2 t.	**onion salt**

Simmer 5 minutes and serve. If thinner soup is desired, add 1 cup more water and season accordingly.

There are but few who realize that in order to enjoy health and cheerfulness, they must have an abundance of sunlight, pure air and exercise. My Life Today, *p. 138.*

TOMATO SOUP

Add, stir and heat in saucepan:

1–48 oz. can tomato juice
1-1/2 t. onion powder
1/16 t. oregano powder
1/2 t. sweet basil
1/4 t. salt or to taste
1/4 t. celery salt

Blend until creamy (1 minute):

1 c. cashews
1 c. water
2–3 T. honey, liquid, (if tomatoes are tart—add honey to taste)

Combine mixtures, sitrring constantly. Bring just to a boil and serve or remove from burner.

In order to know what are the best foods, we must study God's original plan for man's diet. He who created man and who understands his needs appointed Adam his food. "Behold," He said, "I have given you every herb yielding seed, ... and every tree in which is the fruit of a tree yielding seed; to you it shall be for food." Counsels on Diet and Foods, p. 81.

Our Saviour's words, "Come unto Me, ... and I will give you rest," is a prescription for the healing of physical, mental, and spiritual ills. Though men have brought suffering upon themselves by their own wrongdoing He regards them with pity. In Him they may find help. He will do great things for those who trust in Him. My Life Today, p. 155.

Thought for the day

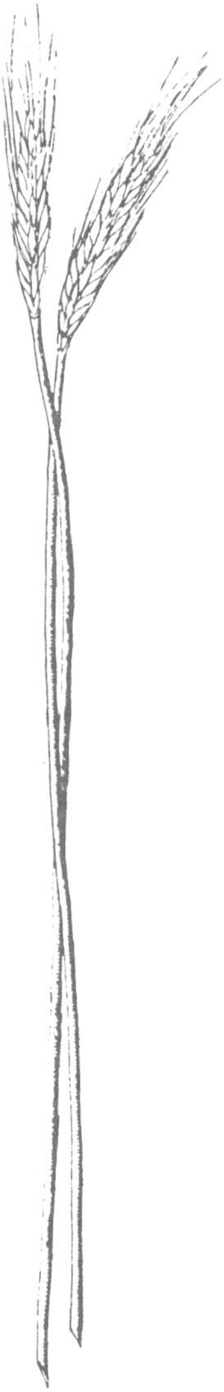

In our home hangs a special picture of an old man bowing his head in prayer, thankful for his meager meal. On the rough table there is a bowl of tomato soup, a small loaf of whole grain bread, an apple, a well worn Bible and a pair of reading glasses.

The old man wears a coarse, wool shirt. It's probably cold out, and he is thankful for his warm soup. It is a picture of gratefulness and faith—a reminder we owe God thanks for every blessing, every morsel of food, every breath of life—because "one died" in our place. If we believe and really appreciate our Saviour's grace, we pause with a heart full of sincere appreciation to say "thank you for your amazing, self-sacrificing love."

"He Himself gives all men life and breath and everything else." Acts 17:25 last part, NIV.

Remember God loves you and every gift is yours.

Notes

Seasonings

SUGGESTED SEASONINGS

No harmful effects known

Sweet Herbs, Non-Irritating

Anise seed
Basil/Sweet Basil
Bay leaf
Cardamon
Caraway Seed
Celery Seed
Celery Salt
Chervil
Chives
Coriander
Cumin
Dill seed
Fennel
Fenugreek
Garlic Salt/Powder
Marjoram
Mint
Onion Salt/Powder
Oregano
Paprika (Spanish)
Parsley
Peppermint
Rosemary
Sage
Savory
Spearmint
Tarragon
Thyme
Wintergreen
Engevita Yeast (see p. 2) Flakes
Non-bittered Brewers Yeast Flakes

"The appetite for liquor is encouraged by the preparation of food with condiments and spices .... Foods should be prepared in as simple a manner as possible, free from condiments and spices, and even from an undue amount of salt." *Counsels on Diet and Foods*, p. 339, 340.

TO FREEZE SWEET RED BELL PEPPER

Wash, then place sweet red bell pepper on cookie sheet stem part down. Place in 250° F. oven for 1 hour. Remove from oven, put directly into plastic bag and tie. Let steam in bag about 1 hour. Remove skins and seeds. Freeze individual amounts equal to 1/4 or 1/3 c. portions on cookie sheets. Store each portion when frozen in small freezer bags or containers in freezer for convenient use in recipes. Can be used where pimento is called for in recipes.

A simple remedy for irritability:

- *eat at regular times*
- *nothing between meals but water*
- *allow 5 hours between meals so food can properly digest*

MOCK CHICKEN SEASONING #1

Mix in bowl:

1 T. dried parsley
2 T. dried green bell pepper*
1 T. dried red bell pepper*
1 T. celery powder**
4 T. onion powder
1 c. Engevita yeast (see p. 2)

Place mixture in blender or small coffee grinder and blend until very fine. Store in air-tight container.

* Chop bell peppers in fine pieces. Dry in low oven (150° F.). Keep stirring every 15 minutes until brittle. Store in air-tight jar.

** To make celery powder, grind celery seed in small coffee grinder until powdery.

MOCK CHICKEN SEASONING #2

Mix well in bowl:

1 c. Engevita yeast (see p. 2)
2 t. onion powder
1 t. onion salt
1/2 t. sage
1/2 t. thyme
1/2 t. marjoram
3 T. parsley flakes
(powder in coffee grinder)*
1-1/2 t. garlic salt
1-1/2 t. celery salt
2 T. dehydrated green bell pepper
(powder in coffee grinder)*
1/4 t. savory

Pour in air-tight jar.
Nice on Scrambled Tofu. (see p. 143)
*Measure parsley flakes and dehydrated green bell pepper before powdering in coffee grinder.

LORRAINE'S "ITALIAN SEASONING"

In bowl, add:

1 T. sage
1/4 t. rosemary
1/4 t. oregano
1 T. sweet savory
1 T. thyme

Mix well and keep in air-tight container.

Thanks Lorraine Barker for sharing recipe!

CHILI POWDER

In bowl add:

2 T. paprika
2 T. cumin
1 T. oregano
1 T. garlic powder
1 T. Lorraine's "Italian Seasoning" (see above)

Mix well and keep in air-tight container.

RHONA CLARKE'S IRISH CURRY POWDER

3 T. cumin
2 t. corriander
1 t. tumeric
1/4 t. fenugreek
1/2 t. salt
1/4 t. cardamon

Thanks Rhona Clarke for sharing recipe!

Air, the precious gift of heaven,

... soother of the nerves.
... induces sound and sweet sleep.
Counsels on Health, p. 60.

Thought for the day

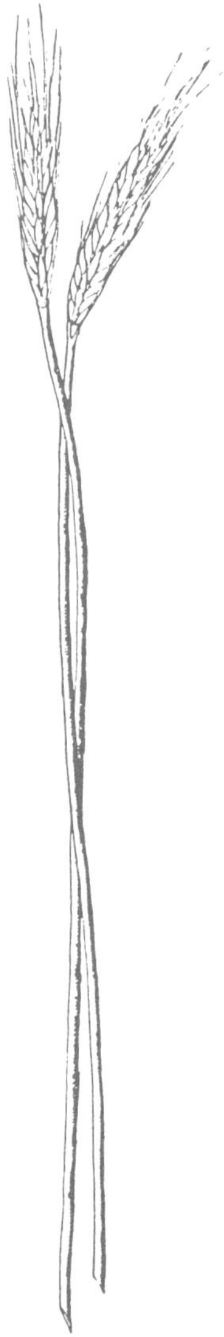

God has given my son and his wife a special talent for finding novel ways of sharing His love. One I treasure is a pretty, little spice container. The spice is "LOVE". Underneath it says, "Spice for Living," net weight "Immeasurable." On the side, written in wedgewood blue, is the word "LOVE"—ingredients: "Faithfulness, Gentleness, Goodness, Joy, Kindness, Patience, Peace, Perseverance, Protection, Trust, Truthfulness and Unselfishness."

"Love" is a very special spice needed in every recipe. Use it freely in every recipe "and live a life of love, just as Christ loved us and gave himself up for us as a fragrant offering and sacrifice to God." Ephesians 5:2 NIV. Only a response of love makes any lasting changes and will give of its best. Jesus, while on earth said to His followers, "Ye are the salt of the earth." Matthew 5:13.

"The savor of the salt represents the love of Jesus in the heart....If it is dwelling in us, it will flow out to others..." (*Thoughts from the Mount of Blessing*, p. 36) with unselfish love.

Remember, God loves you.

Notes

Breakfast

Breakfast

"EAT A SUBSTANTIAL BREAKFAST"

"Make your breakfast correspond more nearly to the heartiest meal of the day." *Counsels on Diet and Foods*, p. 173.

Avoid "stereotyped breakfasts"—porridge—the same thing every day...your family will "come to dread" the meal "which should be interesting to them." *Ibid.*, p. 259.

"...take something warm into the stomach, every morning..." *Ibid.*, p. 86.

Vary the meals from day to day.

Different Breads	e.g. whole wheat, rye, cornbread, raisin bread, muffins, date nut and raisin roll, etc.
Cooked Cereals	millet pudding, baked oatmeal, brown rice, cornmeal, etc.
Whole grain	waffles, pancakes, crepes, with fruit sauces
Home-made Granola .	or "Shredded Wheat" (cereal) with "Grapenuts" (cereal) occasionally

Note: The Breakfast Banana Split (see p. 133) for something special!

WHY BREAKFAST IS SO IMPORTANT

1. Supplies energy—after a long night's rest.
2. Stops the urge to snack.
3. Prevents irritability and fatigue.
4. Promotes better attitudes and scholastic attainment.
5. Weight control—by promoting regular meals.
6. Helps stabilize blood sugar levels.
7. Improves efficiency and safety.

VITAMIN B1 (THIAMINE)
—for healthy nerves

Good Sources of Thiamine:
Whole grains: especially buckwheat, Bulgar wheat (see p. 1), cornmeal, millet, oats, rye (whole), wheat (whole grain), wheat bran, wheatgerm, wild rice, rice polishings, popcorn.

Nuts: almonds, Brazil nuts, cashews, dried chestnuts, filberts, raw peanuts, pecans, English walnuts, peanut butter.

Whole Sesame and Sunflower Seeds
Brewers yeast, Torula yeast, Engevita yeast (see p. 2)
Legumes: dried beans, garbanzos (chick peas), kidney beans, green peas, soybeans, green split peas, lentils

Baked potatoes with skin, Asparagus

Avoid over-cooking and remember baking powder and soda destroy some thiamine (B_1).

RICH ALMOND CASHEW MILK

Blend in blender until creamy (1 minute):

1/3 c. cashews, raw
1/3 c. almonds, blanched
1 c. water

Add and blend:

1 T. honey, liquid
3 c. water
1/8 t. salt

For CREAM, omit 1 cup water. Refrigerate.

By neglecting to take physical exercise, by overworking mind or body, we unbalance the nervous system. Counsels on Health, p. 41.

RICH ALMOND RICE MILK

Blend in blender until creamy (1 minute):

1/2 c. almonds, blanched
1/2 c. water

Add and blend (1 minute):

1/2 c. water

Add and blend:

1/4 t. salt
1 c. white rice, "Uncle Ben's" converted, cooked and salted
2 T. honey, liquid
2 t. vanilla
1-1/2 c. water

Refrigerate.

CASHEW MILK

Blend in blender until creamy (1 minute):

2/3 c. cashews, raw
2/3 c. water

Add and blend:

3 c. water
1 T. honey, liquid
1/8 t. salt or to taste
1 t. vanilla

Place in container and refrigerate.

CASHEW CREAM

Blend in blender until creamy (1 minute):

1/2 c. cashews, raw
1/2 c. water

Add and blend:

pinch of salt
2 t. honey or to taste
1/4 t. vanilla
1/4 c. water

Place in container and refrigerate.

SOY MILK CONCENTRATE

Soak **2-1/4 cups soybeans** overnight.
Drain.
Yeilds 4-1/2 c. soaked soybeans.
Pour hot tap water over beans to warm them.

Put in blender:

1-1/2 c. beans, warmed
2 c. water, boiling

Blend for 2 minutes. Repeat until all the beans are used (or freeze some of the beans for later use).

Strain through nylon cloth or bag. Knead until all the milk is extracted.

Cook the strained milk in double boiler for 30 minutes.

When cold add:

Equal parts water
1 T. honey, liquid
1/4 t. salt
1 t. vanilla

Thanks Donalea Strunk for sharing recipe!

NUT FRENCH TOAST

Blend in blender until creamy (1 minute):

1/2 c. almonds
1/4 c. cashews
3/4 c. water

Add and blend:

3/4 c. water
1 t. arrowroot powder
1/2 t. salt

Dip whole wheat bread slices in nut batter. Fry until golden in Silverstone frying pan with a trickle of oil.

A walk, even in winter, would be more beneficial to the health than all the medicine the doctors may prescribe. Counsels on Health, p. 52.

LONG COOKING OF GRAINS

"**Long cooking** improves the nutritive value by breaking chemical bondages which are not broken by shorter cooking nor by the digestive processes."

"Many grains may be used cracked or ground coarsely. Try combining two different grains such as rice and buckwheat. Use as wide a variety as is possible, but do not mix more than two or three grains in one dish. Some of the less common grains are: Red whole wheat, rye (both rolled and whole grain), oat groats, **Brown Rice, Buckwheat Groats**, hulled barley, hulled **Millet**, and milo maize. Whole kernel cereals should be cooked for several hours. General directions are: 1 cup cereal, 1/2 teaspoon salt, and 3–4 cups water..."

Thank you Dr. Agatha Thrash for sharing.

DEXTRINIZED GRAINS OR FLOUR

Dextrinizing (see p. 2) grains or flour will shorten their cooking times and improve their flavor.

Uncooked whole grains such as rice, wheat kernels (berries), rye, oats, cornmeal, cracked wheat, etc. are dextrinized by heating the grain in a heavy skillet until very light brown in color. Stir constantly on moderately high heat for 3–5 minutes.

Wholegrain kernels will not necessarily brown, but will make a popping noise when heated.

THREE GRAIN CROCK POT CEREAL

Bring to boil in pot :

3 c. water

Add and boil 1 minute:

2/3 c. oat flakes
1/3 c. rye flakes
1/3 c. wheat flakes
1/4 t. salt

Rinse crock pot with hot water, plug in on low and add above ingredients. Cook overnight or at least 7 hours.

Serve with nutmilk or soymilk.
For added nutrition, sprinkle on a few chopped nuts or seeds.

MILLET SEED CROCK POT CEREAL

Bring to boil in pot:

3 c. water

Add and boil 1 minute:

1/2 c. millet
1/2 c. oat flakes, large (regular)
1 T. sesame seeds
1/4 t. salt

Rinse crock pot with hot water, plug in on low and add above ingredients.

Cook overnight or at least 7 hours.
Serve with nutmilk or soymilk.
For added nutrition, sprinkle on a few chopped nuts or seeds.

CROCK POT MILLET

Cook only in 1 quart, 1 temperature crock pot.
In crock pot:

1/2 c. millet
1/4 t. salt
2-1/4 c. water

Optional: 1/4 c. Sultana raisins, washed; 1/4 c. dates, chopped; figs or apricots in same proportions. When using dried fruit, add 1/3 c. more water to above recipe.

Plug in crock pot on low and cook overnight or at least 7 hours.
Serve with nutmilk or soymilk.
For added nutrition, sprinkle on a few chopped nuts or seeds.

Thanks Carol-Ann Nelson for sharing recipe!

CROCK POT BUCKWHEAT

Cook only in 1 quart, 1 temperature crock pot.
In crock pot:

1/2 c. buckwheat groats (see p. 130)
1/4 t. salt
1-2/3 c. water

Optional: 1/4 c. chopped walnuts; 2 or 3 chopped Calamyrna figs.

When using dried fruit in the recipe, add 1/3 c. more water. Plug in crock pot on low.

Cook overnight or at least 6 hours.

Thanks Carol-Ann Nelson for sharing recipe!

CROCK POT CORNMEAL

Cook only in 1 quart, 1 temperature crock pot.
Lightly brush crock pot with Home Spray (see p. 148) or oil.
In crock pot:

2/3 c. cornmeal
1/4 t. salt
2-3/4 c. water
4 *or* 6 dried apricots, chopped
4 sections dried pears, chopped

Plug in crock pot on low and cook overnight or at least 7 hours.

Thanks Carol-Ann Nelson for sharing recipe!

BUCKWHEAT GROATS

Bring 2-1/2 c. water to boil in pot.

Add: **1/4 t. salt**
1 c. buckwheat groats

Lower heat to lowest setting. Simmer for 20 minutes.

COOKED CORNMEAL

In saucepan:

4 c. water, cold
1 c. cornmeal
1/2 t. salt

Stir frequently while thickening or until it comes to a boil. Lower to lowest setting—and simmer 20 minutes.

Optional: add 2 or 3 T. unsweetened shredded coconut while cooking.

APPLE MILLET

In casserole combine:

1/2 c. millet seed, hulled
2 apples, washed, peeled and sliced
1/2 c. Sultana raisins, washed
1/4 t. salt
1-3/4 c. water, boiling
1/4 c. apple concentrate (undiluted, frozen apple juice)
or **1/4 c. more water**

Blend in blender until creamy:

3 T. almonds, blanched
1/4 c. water

Mix all together—and mix well. Bake at 350° F. for 1 hour.

Thankful hearts and kind looks are more valuable than wealth and luxury, and contentment with simple things will make home happy if love be there. The Adventist Home, p. 108.

MILLET PUDDING

Mix in casserole:

	1 c.	**millet seed, hulled**
	1/2 c.	**dates, chopped**
	1/2 c.	**Sultana raisins, washed**
	1/2 t.	**salt**
Add:	**4 c.**	**water, boiling**
Optional—Add:	**1 t.**	**vanilla**

Mix well, bake in 350° F. oven for 1 hour.

For special treat—serve with toasted, sliced almonds on top. Serve with soymilk or nutmilk.

MILLET PUDDING VARIATION

Mix in casserole:

	1 c.	**millet seed, hulled**
	1/3 c.	**Sultana raisins, washed**
	1/3 c.	**currants, washed**
	1/3 c.	**dried apricots, chopped**
	1/2 t.	**salt**
Add:	**4 c.**	**water, boiling**

Mix well. Bake in 350° F. oven for 1 hour.

Thanks Josie Jarnevic for Millet Variation recipe!

The things of nature are God's blessings, provided to give health to body, mind, and soul.... The pure air, the glad sunshine, the beautiful flowers and trees, the orchards and vineyards, and outdoor exercise amid these surroundings are health giving—the elixir of life. Nothing so tends to restore health and happiness as living amid attractive country surroundings. My Life Today, p. 135.

BREAKFAST BANANA SPLIT

Use suitable banana split dishes.

Add: **2 ice-cream scoops of cooked oatmeal**
banana, sliced (as in a banana split)

Topping suggestions:

strawberries , slightly thickened
blueberries, sweetened and slightly thickened

Sprinkle nuts over topping.

JOAN'S OATMEAL CEREAL

Bring to boil in saucepan:

4 c. water
1/2 t. salt
2/3 c. dates, chopped
1/2 c. raisins

Lower heat and simmer for 10 minutes.

Add: **2 c. oat flakes, large (regular)**

Simmer 15 minutes more. It's special!

Thanks Joan Barker for sharing recipe!

BAKED OATMEAL

Mix in casserole:

2-1/2 c. oat flakes, large (regular)
1 c. Sultana raisins, washed
2 apples, sliced
2 bananas, sliced

Bring to boil and mix with above:

4 c. water
1/2 t. salt

Bake at 350° F. for 1 hour. Serve in bowls with soymilk or nutmilk.

Optional: **1 t. vanilla**
1/2 c. coconut, unsweetened and shredded

"OATS-WHEAT-RYE" FLAKES CEREAL

In pot:

2 c. water to boil
1/4 t. salt

Add: **1/3 c. rye flakes**
1/3 c. oat flakes
1/3 c. wheat flakes

Bring to boil then lower heat to lowest and simmer 15–20 min.

Optional—Add 1/2 c. washed Sultana raisins to water.

RAISIN SAUCE

Suggestion: Brown rice with Raisin Sauce
or
Any plain cereal with Raisin Sauce

In pot:

2-1/4 c. water
2 c. Sultana raisins, washed

Simmer until plump.

Add: **1 t. vanilla** *or* **a little maple flavoring, or to taste**
1/8 t. salt
1 T. honey, liquid

Thicken with 2 T. arrowroot powder and 1/4 c. water. Stir until thick. Serve over plain hot cereal.

Thanks Joan Barker for sharing recipe!

The better you observe the laws of health, the more clearly can you discern temptations, and resist them, and the more clearly you can discern the value of eternal things. *My Life Today*, *p. 141.*

RED RIVER CEREAL AND DATES

In pot:

3 c. water to boil
1/4 t. salt

Add: **1/2 c. dates, chopped**
1 c. "Red River Cereal" (a multi-grain brand of cereal)

Bring to boil then lower heat.
Stir occasionally. Simmer on low heat 20 minutes.
Delicious with soy or nutmilk and sliced bananas!

PLAIN BROWN RICE

(Favorite: Lundberg Short Grain Brown Rice)

Bring to boil—in saucepan:

2 c. water
1/4 t. salt

Wash:

1 c. + 2 T. brown rice and add to water

Bring to boil and simmer for 40 minutes.

WHITE BASMATI RICE

Same method as above except simmer 20 minutes.

It's the little things which reveal the chapters of the heart. It is the little attentions, the numerous small incidents and simple courtesies of life, that make up the sum of life's happiness;.... The Adventist Home, p. 108.

...all are to find their happiness in the happiness of those whom they help and bless. Our High Calling, p. 164.

BREAKFAST RICE

Blend in blender till creamy (1 minute):

3 T. almonds, blanched
1/4 c. water

When blended, add:

2/3 c. water
1/4 t. salt

In casserole, add the above ingredients.
Then add:

1 c. brown rice (Lundberg)
1-1/2 c. water, boiling
1 banana, sliced
1/4 t. pure vanilla
1/3 c. Sultana raisins, washed
2 T. currants, washed*

*or omit currants and use 1/2 c. Sultana raisins instead of 1/3 c. Mix lightly. Bake at 350° F. for 1 hour.

BAKED WHOLE WHEAT KERNELS

Bake day ahead and reheat—half recipe enough for family of four. Bake full recipe and have it two different mornings, two different ways.

Check kernels (berries) for any foreign matter and wash.
Preheat oven to 275° F.
In casserole:

1-1/2 c. wheat kernels (berries), soft
3-1/2 c. water, boiling
1/2 t. salt

Cover with lid. Bake at 275° F. for 4 hours.
Reheat in double boiler:

half the baked kernels
1/2 c. water
1/3 c. dates, chopped

Simmer in double boiler 1 hour.

continued...

or **half the baked kernels**
1/2 c. water
1/3 c. Sultana raisins, washed

Simmer in double boiler 1 hour.

PANCAKES

Blend in blender until creamy (1 minute):

1/3 c. almonds, unblanched
1/2 c. water

Add to blender while blending:

2 c. water
1-1/4 c. tofu, crumbled firm
1/2 c. "Cream of Wheat" dry cereal
1/2 c. cornmeal
3/4 t. salt
1 T. honey, liquid
1 c. oats, quick

When blender starts to work hard—pulsate or just turn off and on again. Let sit 5 minutes. Add a trickle of oil on Silverstone frying pan. Drop batter by ladle to desired size and fry until golden on each side.

Note: Electric frying pan setting is 300° F.

"BON MILLET" PANCAKES

Blend in blender until creamy:

1/3 c. almonds
1/2 c. water

Add: **1/2 t. salt**
3/4 c. millet flour
2-1/2 c. water
1 c. tofu, crumbled
1/2 c. cornmeal
1/2 c. oats, quick

Optional: **1 T. honey, liquid**

Blend well. Let sit 5 minutes.
Drop by large spoonfuls on lightly greased Silverstone frying pan. Fry approximately 5 minutes on each side.

ALMOND OAT WAFFLES

Blend in blender until creamy (1 minute):

1/3 c. almonds, raw
1/2 c. water

Add and blend:

2 c. water
1-1/2 c. oats, quick
1/2 t. salt
1/4 c. bran
1 T. sesame seeds, unhulled

Let stand 5 minutes for oats to absorb moisture. Grease waffle iron with Home Spray (see p. 148) (brushed on) and preheat. Add batter and bake 10–12 minutes on medium-high (depends on waffle iron). Do not open lid before the time is up.

SUNNY ALMOND WAFFLES

Blend in blender until creamy (1 minute):

1/4 c. almonds
2 T. sunflower seeds
1/2 t. salt
1 t. vanilla
1/2 c. water

Add and blend, then let stand 5 minutes:

2 c. water
1-1/2 c. oats, quick
2 T. bran
4 dates *(optional)*

Prepare a non-stick waffle iron with Home Spray (see p. 148). Pour on batter. Bake on medium-high heat for 10–12 minutes or until waffle is done. Do not open waffle iron until waffle is done. Cooking time depends on waffle iron as heat varies in different makes. Omit dates for lighter colored, unsweetened waffles.

GARBANZO OAT WAFFLES

Clean, sort and wash beans.
Soak overnight:

1/2 c. dry garbanzos (chick peas) (1 c. soaked)

Blend in blender until creamy:

1 c. garbanzos, soaked
1 c. water

Add and blend:

1-1/2 c. water
1-1/2 c. oats, quick
1/2 t. salt
1 t. vanilla

Optional: **1 T. honey, liquid** (will turn waffle dark and sweet).

Let stand 5 minutes for oats to absorb moisture. Grease waffle iron with Home Spray (see p. 148) (brushed on) and preheat on medium-high.

Add batter and bake 10–12 minutes (depends on waffle iron). Do not open lid before the time is up.

SUNFLOWER SEED WAFFLES
(or pumpkin seeds!)

Blend in blender until creamy (1 minute):

1/3 c. sunflower seeds
1/2 c. water

Add and blend:

2 c. water
1-1/2 c. oats, quick
1/2 t. salt
1/4 c. bran

Let stand 5 minutes for oats to absorb moisture. Grease waffle iron with Home Spray (see p. 148) (brushed on) and preheat on medium-high. Add batter and bake 10–12 minutes, depending on waffle iron.

Do not open lid before time is up.

SOYA OAT WAFFLES

Clean, sort and wash beans.
Soak overnight—desired amount of soybeans:

1/2 c. dry soybeans (this equals about 1 c. when soaked)

Blend in blender until creamy:

1 c. soybeans, soaked
1 c. water

Add and blend:

1-1/2 c. water
1-1/2 c. oats, quick
1/2 t. salt
1 t. vanilla

Blend until satiny.

Optional: **1 T. honey, liquid** (will turn waffle dark and sweet).

Let stand 5 minutes for oats to absorb moisture.
Grease waffle iron with Home Spray (see p. 148) (brushed on) and preheat on medium-high.

Add batter and bake 10–12 minutes (depends on waffle iron). Do not open lid before the time is up.

SPECIAL WAFFLES

Blend in blender until creamy:

1/3 c. sunflower seeds
1/2 c. water

Add to blender while blending:

2-1/2 c. water
1/2 c. cornmeal
1/4 c. sesame seeds
3/4 t. salt
1-1/2 c. oats, quick
1/4 c. bran
1/2 c. water

continued...

Optional: **1 T. honey, liquid**

Note: The waffles are light without the honey —dark with honey. Let batter sit 5 minutes.

Pour in greased, preheated (medium-high) waffle iron for 12 minutes.

For a new flavor—instead of 2-1/2 c. water, use 2-1/2 c. apple juice. Don't use honey with this combination.

TOASTED SESAME SOY WAFFLES

Soak overnight—desired amount of soybeans:

1/2 c. dry soybeans (this equals about 1 c. when soaked)

Blend in blender until very creamy (2 minutes):

1 c. soybeans, soaked (above)
1 c. water
1 t. vanilla
4 dates *(optional)*

Add and blend, then let stand 5 minutes:

1-1/2 c. water
1-1/2 c. oats, quick
2 T. bran
1 t. salt

Prepare a non-stick wafle iron with Home Spray (see p. 148). Sprinkle the hot waffle iron with unhulled sesame seeds, pour on batter, then sprinkle more sesame seeds on top. Bake on medium-high heat for 10–12 minutes or until done. Do not open waffle iron until waffle is done. Cooking time depends on the waffle iron as heat varies in different makes. Omit dates for lighter colored, unsweetened waffles.

Optional: Use raw garbanzos, soaked overnight in water in place of soybeans.

Let the table be made inviting and attractive, as it is supplied with the good things which God has so bountifully bestowed. Let mealtime be a cheerful, happy time. As we enjoy the gifts of God, let us respond by grateful praise to the Giver. My Life Today, p. 132.

GRANOLA

Mix in large bowl all dry ingredients:

6 c. oat flakes, large (regular)
2 c. oats, quick
1 c. coconut, unsweetened and shredded
2/3 c. wheat germ
1/4 c. sesame seeds, unhulled
2/3 c. almonds, sliced
2/3 c. pecans *or* **nut of choice** *or* **sunflower seeds, chopped**
1/2 c. cornmeal
1/4 c. flour, whole wheat
1 t. salt

In small pitcher:

1-1/3 c. orange juice, frozen, thawed from concentrate
1 t. vanilla

Pour liquid over dry ingredients and mix well by tumbling through fingers.

Divide on 2 Silverstone cookie sheets that fit in oven together. Bake at 250° F. for 1-1/2 hours. Stir every 30 minutes. Remove from oven and let cool on rack. When cool add dried fruits of choice-such as raisins, apricots, etc. Put in container to store.

CHUNKY FRUIT GRANOLA

In large bowl:

6 c. oat flakes, large (regular)
1/2 c. rye flakes
1/2 c. oat bran
1 c. almonds, sliced
1/2 c. sesame seeds
1 c. coconut, unsweetened and shredded
3/4 t. salt

continued...

Blend in blender until creamy:

1/2 c. pineapple juice, unsweetened
1/2 c. pineapple, dehydrated

Add: **1/4 c. more pineapple juice**
1/2 c. oil

Pour liquids over dry ingredients and mix well tumbling through fingers. Divide on 2 Silverstone cookie sheets that fit in oven together. Bake at 250° F. for 1-1/2 hours; stirring every 30 minutes. Remove from oven and cool on rack.

When Granola is cool, add:

1/2 c. papaya chunks, small
1/2 c. Sultana raisins

Store in container. Very rich. Eat sparingly or as a topping on plain cooked cereals.

Note: If you have a dehydrator, dehydrate your own pineapple, e.g. unsweetened dessert bits.

SCRAMBLED TOFU

In Silverstone frying pan, add 1 t. oil.
To each cube (1 cup crumbled tofu), add:

1/4 t. garlic salt
1/4 t. onion salt
2 t. Mock Chicken Seasoning #2 (see p. 119) or to taste

Add a small dash of tumeric, if desired, to give yellow color.

Option #1: Sauté onions, then follow above recipe. Salt to taste.
Option #2: Sauté green pepper and 1 firm tomato, cut up—then follow above recipe. Salt to taste.

FRUIT TOAST

Drain canned fruit. Thicken the syrup. Fold the fruit into the thickened syrup.

Serve on toast.
As a special treat put Almond Butter (see p. 172) on toast; then top with thickened fruit.

BLUEBERRY TOAST

In pot: **2 c. blueberries, frozen**
pinch of salt
1/2 c. grape juice
sweeten to taste
1 t. lemon juice

Thicken with:

2 T. cornstarch mixed in **1/4 c. grape juice**

Serve on toast.

APPLE SAUCE

Wash, peel, slice:

6 c. apples

Add: **1/2 c. apple juice, frozen then thawed**

Bring to boil and lower heat to simmer until done (depends on apples).

Optional: Add 1/2 c. washed raisins during the last few minutes of cooking.

Suggested Breakfast: Toast with Whipped Peanut Butter (see p. 173), and cover with hot Apple Sauce.

DRIED FRUIT SAUCE

In pot: **2 c. apple juice**
4 apples, chopped

Bring to boil, then lower heat and simmer 15 minutes.

Add: **2 c. apple juice**
1/2 c. dried apricots, chopped
1/2 c. Sultana raisins, washed
1 c. dried prunes, pitted and cut up
pinch of salt

Bring to boil, lower heat and simmer 15 minutes longer.

Optional: Just before serving, heat and serve on cooked cereal instead of milk.

Optional: Add sliced bananas or frozen strawberries.

Thought for the day

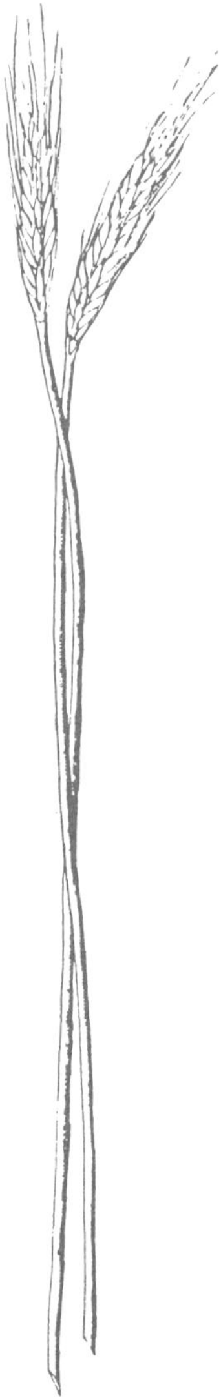

Breakfast means "breaking the fast." It's a time to enjoy God's bounties and get energy for the day.

A PRAYER FOR DAILY BREAD

"Give us this day our daily bread;"
For by Thy goodness we are fed.
To Israel manna Thou didst send,
So on Thy bounty we depend.

But what does daily manna mean?
Is it only food that can be seen
And eaten with a spoon and fork—
The only food for which we work?

No! Man lives not alone by bread,
But by the Word of God is fed.
Christ and His Word, they satisfy;
Who eats this Bread shall never die.

Harold A. Toms,
March 13, 1989

Remember, God loves you.

Notes

Breads & Crackers

LIVE YEAST AND HOT YEAST BREADS

Live yeast cells can pass through the stomach acids without destruction and later grow in the intestines, causing fermentation and destroying B vitamins from the food materials in the intestines.

Brewer's yeast does not present these problems since the yeast cells have been killed in the drying process and do not destroy the vitamin B in the food present in the intestines. Brewer's yeast flakes and other food yeasts are very good sources of Vitamin B.

Yeast-raised foods should be thoroughly baked and they are best eaten after being cooled 12 to 24 hours. They may be reheated if desired.

Back of the bread is the fluffy flour
And back of the flour the mill
And back of the mill is the wheat and the shower
And the sun and the Father's will.

From—"Getting It Together L.25", Bessie Mae Bellinghausen

When yeast-raised bread is sliced and dried in a warm oven (around 300 degrees) till crunchy crispy, it will keep for a longer time and is called zwieback.

The staff of life—needs to be made from nutritious ingredients and a variety of whole grains.

HOME SPRAY—To Grease Pans, casserole dishes, etc.

Put in spray bottle, spray and brush on!

1 c. corn oil
1 T. liquid soy lecithin

Mix well by shaking. Spray lightly and brush on—nothing sticks!

BREADS—COMMON DEFECTS AND POSSIBLE CAUSES

1. **SOUR TASTE**
   a. Water too warm.
   b. Period of rising too long, especially in whole grain breads which will not rise as light as white breads.
   c. Temperature too high while rising.
   d. Poor yeast.
2. **DRY OR CRUMBLY**
   a. Too much flour in dough.
   b. Over-baking.
3. **HEAVINESS**
   a. Unevenness of temperature while rising.
   b. Insufficient kneading.
   c. Old flour.
   d. Old yeast.
4. **CRACKS IN CRUST**
   a. Cooling in a draft.
   b. Baking before sufficiently light.
   c. Oven too hot at first.
5. **TOO THICK A CRUST**
   a. Oven too slow.
   b. Baked too long.
   c. Excess of salt.
6. **DARK PATCHES OR STREAKS**
   a. Poor materials.
   b. Shortening added to flour before liquid, thus allowing flour particles to become coated with fat before they had mixed evenly with the liquid.
7. **SOGGINESS**
   a. Too much liquid.
   b. Insufficient baking.
   c. Cooling in airtight container.
8. **ILL-SHAPED LOAF**
   a. Not molded well originally.
   b. Too large a loaf for the pan.
   c. Rising period too long.
   d. Failure to rise to greatest size in oven.
   e. Loaves flat on top may result from inadequate kneading.
9. **COARSE GRAIN**
   a. Too high temperature during rising.
   b. Rising too long or proofing too long.
   c. Oven too cool at first.
   d. Pan too large for size of loaf.
   e. Too much liquid.

From *"Eat For Strength"* by Agatha M. Thrash M.D., p. 13, with permission. Thank you Dr. Thrash for sharing.

BOSCH BREAD (without oil)

Grind in a flour mill (Magic Mill II or III):

9+ c. wheat kernels (berries), whole
1/2 c. rye kernels

Blend in blender:

1/3 c. sunflower seeds
2/3 c. water

Pour liquid in large measuring cup.
Warm on stove:

2-1/2 c. apple juice

Add to blended sunflower seeds.
Add sufficient water to apple juice and blended seeds to equal a scant 7 c.

Pour all the liquid into the Bosch bowl.

Add: **4 c. flour, freshly ground above**
1/3 c. gluten flour
3-1/2 t. salt
2-1/2 T. yeast

Keep adding flour until the bottom half of the bowl is clear (any more and you will have dry bread).

Knead 8 minutes—the bowl will be clear. If after 2 minutes kneading it's not clearing, add 1 or 2 T. of flour. Preheat oven to 150° F.
When time is up on kneading, put on oiled board and shape into loaves in small loaf pans, that have been greased with Home Spray (see p. 148).

Proof in oven at 150° F. for 30 minutes.
Turn oven to 350° F. and bake for 30 minutes for small loaves and 45 minutes for larger loaves.

The Creator of man has arranged the living machinery of our bodies. Every function is wonderfully and wisely made. And God has pledged Himself to keep this human machinery in healthful action if the human agent will obey His laws and co-operate with God. My Life Today, p. 127.

BOSCH WHOLE WHEAT BREAD

Preheat oven to 150° F.
Grind fresh approximately :

10 c. wheat kernels (berries), whole
1/2 c. rye kernels

Blend till creamy, 1 minute:

1/3 c. cashews, raw
1/3 c. water

When smooth, add:

1/3 c. dates, chopped
2/3 c. water

Blend till creamy.

Add: **4 c. more warm water**

Pour liquid into Bosch bowl. Start mixing on #1 speed.

Add: **4 c. flour, whole wheat, freshly ground**
1/3 c. gluten flour
3-1/2 t. salt
2-1/2 T. yeast

Add balance of flour until dough pulls away from the bottom half of the bowl.

Continue blending for 8 to 10 minutes.
Remove from bowl, place on oiled board and shape into small loaves. Put in loaf pans greased with Home Spray (see p. 148).

Place bread in preheated oven at 150° F. for 30 minutes. (Don't turn the oven off.)
If there is room in the oven, place a small pan of water somewhere in oven but not under bread.

When bread is risen, bake at 350° F. for 30 minutes for small loaves and 45 minutes for larger loaves (more time depending on size of loaf).

Air is the free blessing of heaven, calculated to electrify the whole system. My Life Today, p. 137.

HOME MADE BREAD

In bowl:

2 c. water, warm
1 T. brown sugar
2-1/2 T. yeast

Let rise till bubbly.
Mix grains in large bowl:

7 c. flour, whole wheat
5 c. flour, white unbleached
1 c. millet flour (grind in coffee grinder)
1 c. wheat germ
1 c. oats, quick

In pitcher, mix:

5 c. water, warm
4 t. salt
1/4 c. honey, liquid
1/4 c. oil

Mix liquid in with grains. Add yeast mixture to grains. Knead well, adding enough flour to make a dough ball.
Knead 15 minutes by clock. Cover with towel. Let rise till double. Punch down and shape into loaves. Put in bread pans. Let rise till double again. Bake in 350° F. oven for 45 minutes or more, depending on size of loaf pans.

BARKER BUNS—A Bosch Recipe

Grind flours. Preheat oven to 150° F.
Blend in blender, 1 minute:

1/3 c. sunflower seeds
1/2 c. water
2 sm. *or* **1 lg. apple, cored and sliced**
sufficient water to blend smoothly

Pour above in large measuring cup and add warm water to equal 4 c. Blend in blender 2/3 c. chopped dates with equal amounts of some of the above liquid or sufficient to blend smoothly.

Pour all the above liquid ingredients into Bosch bowl.

continued...

Mix and add: **2-1/2 t. salt**
2 c. flour, soft whole wheat
2 c. flour, hard whole wheat
2 T. yeast
1/2 c. gluten flour

Add sufficient flour (half soft and half hard whole wheat in equal proportions) till dough clears from bottom half of bowl. Knead 8 minutes.

Remove dough from Bosch and put in large, greased bowl. Let rise 25 minutes. Just punch down. Form dinner rolls to fill each muffin cup half full as they rise to double in size or more. Place in greased Silverstone muffin tins. Put in preheated oven at 150° F. and leave oven on to raise the buns the second time till double in size—about 20 or 25 minutes. Turn oven to 375° F. Bake 12 to 15 minutes or until the bottoms are golden brown.

They are delicious!

Thanks Norm and Joan Barker for sharing recipe!

DATE-NUT AND RAISIN ROLL

In small bowl:
2 c. water, warm
1/4 t. ascorbic acid *(optional)*
1/3 c. honey, liquid
1 T. yeast

Let stand till bubbly.

Add: **1/2 c. oat flour**
1-3/4 c. + 2 rounded T. flour, whole wheat
1 level T. gluten flour
1 t. salt
2 t. vanilla

Mix well and beat about 3 minutes, till well-mixed. Fold in:
1 c. dates, chopped
1 c. raisins
1/2 c. walnuts *or* **pecans, chopped**

Pour into 3 greased tins (19 oz. size) about 1/2 full. Put on a tinfoil top and tie with string to hold on lid. Place in steamer and cook at a gentle, steady boil for 2 hours.

CORN BREAD

In small bowl:

2 T. honey, liquid

Heat till warm in small pot:

1-1/4 c. soymilk *or* nutmilk

Combine honey and soymilk.

Add: **1 T. + 1 t. yeast**

Stir and let rise till bubbly. In large bowl:

1 c. cornmeal
1/2 c. flour, whole wheat
1/2 c. flour, white unbleached
1 t. salt

Add: **1/3 c. oil to yeast mixture**

Add liquids to dry ingredients.
Mix well, beating about 4–5 minutes.
Pour into greased Pyrex dish or pan about 6-1/2" x 8-1/2".
Bake at 350° F. for 25 to 30 minutes or till golden and toothpick comes out dry and clean.

For muffins: Divide dough into 12 muffins and bake in greased Silverstone muffin tins at 350° F. for 20 minutes.

UNLEAVENED FRUIT BREAD

In double boiler:

2 c. water
1 c. cracked wheat
3/4 t. salt

Stir and start timing when water boils in bottom of double boiler. Lower heat to medium boil. Boil 1 hour. Stir every 1/2 hour and check water content in double boiler.

Add: **1 c. Sultana raisins, washed**
1/2 c. dates, chopped
1/2 c. figs, chopped

continued...

Then add:

1/2 c. Almond Butter (see p. 172)
blended with 1/2 c. hot water
1/3 c. honey, liquid

Mix well and continue cooking in double boiler for 1/2 hour. Pour into well greased loaf pan and cover. Bake at 350° F. for 1 hour.

Cool at least 12 hours before slicing. Keep in refrigerator.

Thanks Shirley Laan for sharing recipe!

OAT SCONES

Serve hot, made fresh. In large bowl:

3/4 c. flour, pastry, whole wheat, soft stone-ground
or **1 c. soft wheat** if ground in Magic Mill
1-1/2 c. oats, quick
1/3 c. "Loma Linda Soyagen" powder
1/2 t. salt
3/4 c. Sultana raisins, washed

Emulsify with fork:

1 c. water
1/3 c. oil

Add liquids to dry ingredients and mix well.

Let sit 5 minutes for oats to absorb moisture.

Drop by large tablespoonfuls in a little white, unbleached flour. Roll lightly.

Shape in a ball, then flatten down to 1/4" round scones. Bake on Silverstone cookie sheet at 350° F. for 25–30 minutes, until bottoms are golden.

Serve warm. If eating later, just heat and eat.

FRUIT ROLLS

In small bowl:

1 T. honey, liquid
2 c. water, warm
2 T. yeast

Let rise till bubbly, approximately 5 minutes.

Pour above in big bowl.

Add: **1-1/2 t. salt**
4 c. flour, whole wheat, all-purpose
(1 c. at a time, mixing well)

Pour 1 T. oil in palm of hand and start kneading dough. Add white, unbleached flour a little at a time as needed to knead dough. Knead 15 minutes by the clock. Cover with tea towel till double (30 minutes).

While dough is rising, in small pot:

2 c. dates, cut up
1 c. water

Bring to boil, then lower heat to simmer till creamy, about 10 minutes. Cool.

Wash: **1 c. Sultana raisins**
1/2 c. currants

When dough is double, punch down and knead 1/2 minute. Roll half the dough out in a rectangle approximately 12" x 8". Spread half the date mixture evenly to within 1" of the edges all around.

Sprinkle half the raisins and currants evenly over date mixture. Sprinkle 1/3 c. chopped nuts or desired amount (or none).

Roll the fruit roll lengthwise, slice and place either in a ring or together in greased casserole. Let rise 15 minutes.

Bake in preheated oven at 350° F. for 30 minutes or till dough is golden. With the other half of the dough, shape in small buns and roll in flat circles, putting the date mixture, currants and raisins inside, then tuck them all in well so the fruit is all inside.

Let rise 15 minutes and bake at 350° F. for 25 minutes, depending on size.

See which way you like best!

Delicious wrapped in foil and heated before eating.

APPLE NUT BARS

From "Good Food Party Guide."
In large bowl:

1-1/2 c. oats, quick
3/4 c. dates, chopped
1 t. lemon rind, grated
1/2 t. salt
1/4 c. walnuts, chopped
1/4 c. water
1/4 c. oil
1 c. apple, shredded

Mix well. Press together in 8" x 8" greased pan.
Let stand 10 minutes. Bake at 375° F. for 30 minutes or till golden brown.

Thanks Helen Cate for sharing recipe!

APPLE OAT MUFFINS

In large bowl:

2 c. apple, raw and shredded
3 c. oats, quick
1/3 c. oil
1/2 t. salt
1 c. Sultana raisins, washed
2 T. molasses
1/2 c. dates, chopped fine
1/2 c. walnuts, chopped

Mix well. Let stand 5 minutes to absorb moisture. Shape into 12 muffins by rolling mixture into round balls. They will bake the way you shape them.

Put in greased Silverstone muffin tins or in cupcake wrappers, then into regular muffin tins. Bake at 375° F. for 25 minutes or till bottom of muffin is golden brown.

BANANA DATE MUFFINS

In bowl:

2 c. bananas, ripe mashed
3/4 c. dates, chopped
2/3 c. raisins, washed
1 t. vanilla
1/2 t. salt
1/4 c. oil

Mix well and add:

2-1/4 c. oats, quick
1/2 c. walnuts, chopped
1/4 c. wheat germ
1/4 c. barley flour *or* **oat flour**

Mix well and let stand 10 minutes for oats to absorb liquid. Shape in nice round balls or rounded muffins and place in lightly greased Silverstone muffin tins or in cupcake wrappers in regular muffin tins. (They won't rise, so shape nice and rounded.)

Bake at 350° F. for approximately 45 minutes, depending on the size you make them.

BLUEBERRY MUFFINS

In large bowl:

1 c. Sultana raisins, washed
1 c. blueberries, frozen
2-1/2 c. oats, quick
1/2 t. salt
1/3 c. oil
1 c. apple sauce (see p. 144)

Mix well. Shape into muffins by rolling above mixture into 14 little round balls. There is no baking powder or soda, so they will bake the way you shape them.

Put in greased Silverstone muffin tins. Bake at 350° F. for 30 minutes.

Note: If hands get too sticky while shaping muffins, wash and rinse in cold water—shake well, but don't dry, and it is easier to shape muffins.

BRAN-APPLE MUFFINS

In large bowl:

2-1/4 c. oats, quick
1-1/2 c. bran
3/4 t. salt
1/2 c. walnuts, chopped
1 c. Sultana raisins, washed
2 c. apples, shredded
1/3 c. oil
1/2 c. apple sauce (see p. 144)

Mix well, shaping as desired—they do not rise.
Put in greased Silverstone muffin tins.
Bake at 350° F. for 30 minutes.
Makes 20 muffins.

PINEAPPLE CARROT MUFFINS

In large bowl:

3/4 c. carrot, grated
1 c. pineapple, crushed and unsweetened
1/4 c. coconut, unsweetened and shredded
2-1/2 c. oats, quick
1/2 c. pecans *or* walnuts, chopped
1/2 t. salt
1/3 c. oil *with* 2 T. honey, liquid
1/4 c. oat flour

Mix well.
Shape into muffins by rolling above mixture into 14 little round balls. There is no baking powder or soda, so they will bake the way you shape them.

Put in greased Silverstone muffin tins.
Bake at 350° F. for 30 minutes.

Note: If hands get too sticky while shaping muffins, wash and rinse in cold water—shake well, but don't dry, and it is easier to shape muffins.

TOASTY SESAME OAT BISCUITS

Serve with soup or salad.
In large bowl:

- **3 c. oats, quick**
- **1/4 c. sesame seeds, unhulled**
- **3/4 t. salt**
- **3 T. "Loma Linda Soyagen" Powder** (dry soymilk powder)

Mix well.
In small bowl, emulsify with fork:

- **1/3 c. oil**
- **1 c. water**

Add liquids to dry ingredients and mix well.
Let stand 5 minutes for oats to absorb liquid.
Form into 12 little balls (or 11 bigger) and pat down in 1/4" thick, flat and round biscuits.
Flatten with palm of hands and with fork to shape nicely on Silverstone cookie sheet.

Bake at 350° F. for 30 minutes. Serve warm from oven. Reheat to serve.

OATMEAL CRACKERS—A big recipe!

Mix dry ingredients in a bowl (level measurements):

- **2 c. oats, quick**
- **2 c. flour, pastry, whole wheat**
- **1 c. rye flour**
- **1 c. barley flour**
- **1/2 c. soy flour**
- **1/4 c. wheat germ**
- **1/2 c. coconut, unsweetened and shredded**
- **1/4 c. sesame seeds, ground**
- **1 t. salt**

Emulsify:

- **1-1/4 c. water, cold**
- **1 c. oil**

continued...

Add liquid to dry ingredients and mix well.
Let stand 10 minutes.
Knead a few minutes, then roll out fairly thin on cookie sheet and cut in squares or rectangles.

Bake at 325° F. for approximately 15 minutes or till crisp and crunchy.

The length of baking depends on how thin you have rolled the crackers. The edges of the cookie sheet get done first, so watch closely.

Thanks Joan Barker for sharing recipe!

"CHEEZY" CRACKERS

In large bowl:

1 c. flour, pastry, whole wheat
1 c. oat flour
1/2 t. salt
1/2 t. onion powder
1/4 t onion salt
3 T. Engevita yeast **(see p. 2)**

Emulsify with fork:

1/2 c. corn oil, chilled
1/2 c. water, cold

Add liquids to dry ingredients and mix well.
Roll between wax paper to cracker thickness.
To lift crackers from wax paper, put left hand under the bottom of the bottom layer of wax paper and gently lift crackers off with the right hand.

Cut in squares and prick with a fork.
Put on ungreased Silverstone cookie sheet and bake at 375° F. for 10 to 15 minutes, depending on thickness.

Cool and store in container.

CORN CRACKERS

In large bowl:

1 c. cornmeal
1/3 c. flour, pastry, whole wheat, stone-ground
1/2 c. oat flour
1/2 t. onion powder
1/2 t. salt
1/2 t. onion salt

Bring to boil **2/3 c. water** in small pot.

Add: **1/3 c. oil**

Stir together with fork or whip.
Add liquids to dry ingredients.
Mix well quickly.
Divide dough in half.
Roll out on ungreased Silverstone cookie sheet and score. Bake at 350° F. for 10 minutes or until light golden around the edges or underneath cracker.

Those who make great exertions to accomplish just so much work in a given time, and continue to labor when their judgement tells them they should rest, are never gainers. My Life Today, p. 142.

Perfect health depends upon perfect circulation. Special attention should be given to the extremities, that they may be as thoroughly clothed as the chest and region over the heart. My Life Today, p. 145.

Thought for the day

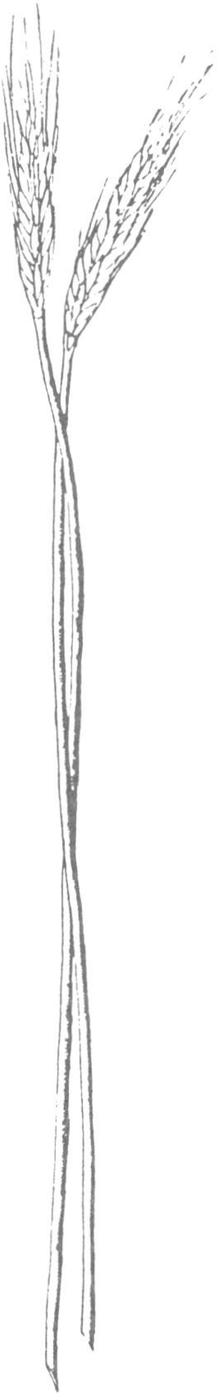

"Why spend money on what is not bread, and your labor on what does not satisfy? Listen, listen to me, and eat what is good, and your soul will delight in the richest fare." Here's our God pleading earnestly with us, "listen, listen to me, and eat what is good" Isaiah 55:2, NIV.

"Beloved, I wish above all things that thou mayest prosper and be in health, even as thy soul prospereth." 3rd John v. 2. There is a close relation between body, mind, thoughts and feelings.

"Cooking may be regarded as less desirable than some other lines of work, but in reality it is a science in value above all other sciences.... The one who understands the art of properly preparing food, and who uses this knowledge, is worthy of higher commendation than those engaged in any other line of work. This talent should be regarded as equal in value to ten talents, for its right use has much to do with keeping the human organism in health. Because so inseparably connected with life and health, it is the most valuable of all gifts." Counsels on Diet and Foods, p. 251.

Remember, God loves you.

Spreads & Sandwiches

THE PROBLEMS OF DIETARY FAT

1. Fats are fattening.
2. Fats affect serum cholesterol.
3. Fats reduce muscular endurance.
4. Fats delay digestion.
5. Fats store poisons.
6. Fats impede circulation.
7. Fats affect cancer.

Used by permission of Gary Strunk.

FATS

"Natural fat as found in cereals, grains and nuts is unsaturated and comes with molecules having a **U** shape. This is called a **Cis** fat. These **U**-shaped molecules are ideal ones for making healthy cell membranes and other vital control chemicals of the body such as prostoglandins, thromboxanes, and lymphokines.

Take the natural oil found in corn. This is **Cis** fat with U-shaped molecules. When oil is extracted from corn and processed, the fat still remains unsaturate. But some of it may be **Trans-fat**. **Trans-fats** make poor cell membranes and may interfere with the chemistry of prostoglandins, thromboxanes, and lymphokines.

It takes about 15 ears of corn to make one tablespoonful of oil. Most refined oils contain between 1% and 19% **Trans-fats**. Modern technology then comes along and hydrogenates or partially hydrogenates these oils. This increases the distortion of the molecules and makes even more **Trans-fats**. Polyunsaturated margarine may contain about one-third of its weight in **Trans-fats**.

Any fat labeled "partially hydrogenated" may have as much as 60% of the provoking **Trans-fats**.

From an article Let's Get Rid of Cancer by
Vernon W. Foster, M.D.

SAUTÉEING VEGETABLES WITHOUT FAT (OR OIL)

Use 1 T. or more water in skillet, as needed. Add chopped vegetables and cook on low or medium heat until tender. Stir as needed. A little extra water may be added if vegetables become too dry during cooking.

"Fats should be kept quite low, ... I would not consider the nut butters, olives, avocado, and other naturally occuring fats as being in this same category.... There is new evidence why margarine may be harmful. Some of the fat in it, although it is all vegetable in origin, has been "hardened" by being saturated with hydrogen. This is true regardless of what margarine is made of. The hydrogenation changes some of the fatty acids into a form called "trans" fatty acids which means that they have different physical properties even though they are the same substance chemically. They have quite a different action in our bodies, and researchers are now finding the "trans" fatty acids block the synthesis of prostaglandins, which are very potent hormones that are anti-inflammatory and prevent blood clotting in the body along with probably other deleterious actions."

Dr. Calvin Thrash

CASHEW PIMENTO CHEESE SPREAD

Blend in blender until creamy (1 minute):

1 c. cashews, raw
1 c. water
2 T. sesame seeds, unhulled

Add and blend as needed for smooth blending:

1 c. water

Add and blend:

1/3 c. sweet red pepper *or* **pimento,** cut in pieces (not pickled)
3/4 t. salt
1/8 t. celery seed
1/4 t. garlic salt
1/4 c. Engevita yeast **(see p. 2)**
2 T. lemon juice, fresh
1 t. onion salt

Add: **1-1/2 T. arrowroot powder** (for soft cheese spread) *or* **2 T. arrowroot powder** (for firm cheese spread)

Put in small pot and bring to boil, stirring constantly. Lower heat and let simmer about 1 minute till thick.

Cool. Put in container and refrigerate.

VELVET CHEESE

This "cheese" can be sliced and has the consistency of American cheese.

Blend till creamy, 1 minute:

1 c. cashews, raw, washed and drained
1-1/4 c. water

While blending, add:

2 T. sesame seeds, unhulled
1/3 c. water
1 t. salt
1-1/4 t. onion salt
1/8 t. celery seed
1/4 t. garlic salt
1/2 lg. pimento (1/4 c. chopped)
3 T. lemon juice

Make a small double boiler (small pot in another saucepan with boiling water).

In small pot:

1/3 c. + 1T. gelatin, "Emes" unflavored
2/3 c. water

Put above pot in saucepan with boiling water.
Heat, stirring frequently, till dissolved.
Pour heated gelatin in with blender ingredients.
Blend quickly and add:

1/4 c. + 1T Engevita yeast (see p. 2)

Blend.
Home Spray (see p. 148) or "Pam" any container and pour Velvet Cheese in it.

Cover and refrigerate.
It takes several hours to set.

MOCKZARELLA CHEESE SPREAD

Blend in blender until creamy, 1 minute:

1-1/2 c. cashews, raw
1-1/2 c. water

continued...

Add and blend:

- **1/2 c. water**
- **3 T. Engevita yeast (see p. 2)**
- **1 t. salt**
- **1 t. onion salt**
- **1/4 c. dried onion flakes**
- **2 T. lemon juice, fresh**
- **1/4 t. garlic powder**
- **2 t. arrowroot powder**

Pour mixture into saucepan.
Cook, stirring constantly, until thick.
Refrigerate.

MOCKZARELLA YOU CAN SLICE

Put in blender:

- **1-1/2 c. cashews, raw, washed**
- **1/4 c. dried onion flakes**
- **1 t. salt**
- **1 t. onion salt**
- **1/4 t. garlic salt**
- **1-1/2 c. water**

Blend till creamy (will get thick quickly).

Fold in : **1/4 c. Engevita yeast (see p. 2)**
2 T. lemon juice, fresh

Pulsate or turn blender on and off, till well-blended and creamy. Make a small double boiler (put a small pot in another saucepan with boiling water).

In smallest pot:

- **1/3 c. + 1 T. gelatin, "Emes" unflavored**
- **1/2 c. water**

This will be thick, but will dissolve when put in saucepan of boiling water (as double boiler). When mixture becomes liquid, pour heated gelatin in with blender ingredients. Blend quickly or pulsate (turn blender on and off).

Home Spray (see p. 148) or "Pam" any container. Pour Mockzarella in. Cover and refrigerate. It takes several hours to set. Will slice.

"NO CHEESE" CHEDDAR-LIKE SPREAD

Blend in blender till creamy:

1/2 c. water
1/3 c. pimento
1 t. salt
1 t. garlic powder
1 t. onion powder
1 t. celery salt
1/4 c. Engevita yeast (see p. 2)
2 T. lemon juice
1/4 c. + 1 T. tomato paste
1/4 c. + 1 T. water

Put in bowl. Fold in:

1 c. tahini (unhulled sesame seed butter)
2/3 c. barley flour

Bake at 350° F. for 30 minutes or till set and firm.

Thanks Bert and Vena Hayward for sharing recipe!

GARBANZO SPREAD

Mix: **2 c. garbanzos (chick peas), cooked, lightly-salted, drained and mashed**

1/3–1/2 c. Soy Mayonnaise (see p. 83)
1/4 t. sweet basil
1/8 t. onion salt
1/8 t. garlic powder
1/4 t. marjoram
1/8 t. rosemary, powdered*
1 t. Mock Chicken Seasoning #1 (see p. 119)

*Grind rosemary in small coffee grinder.

GARLIC SPREAD

Cook until thick:

1 c. water
1/4 c. cornmeal
1/4 t. salt

Blend in blender until creamy (1 minute):

1/4 c. cashews, raw
1/4 c. water
1/2 t. garlic salt
1/2 t. onion powder
1/4 t. salt
2 T. Engevita yeast (see p. 2)

Add and blend:

1/4 c. water and **hot cooked cornmeal**

Refrigerate. For garlic bread use above recipe and add:

1/4 t. garlic powder or to taste

Spread on bread slices and broil until crusty golden.

SUNNY TOMATO SPREAD

Blend in blender till creamy:

2 c. tomatoes, juicy, home canned
or **tomato juice**
1-1/2 T. Engevita yeast (see p. 2)
1/4 t. garlic salt
2 t. onion powder
1 t. Marmite *or* **Savorex,** dissolved in a little of the above mixture, heated in a small pot
2/3 c. sunflower seeds
1/4 t. celery salt
2 T. oats, quick (for a soft spread)
or **1/4 c. for a firmer spread**

Pour in a small greased Pyrexdish. Bake at 350° F. for 45 minutes, uncovered. When cool, refrigerate. Tasty on sandwiches or as a bread spread. May add chopped olives, if desired, for sandwiches.

SAVORY WALNUT SPREAD

Blend (in mini blender) until creamy:

1/2 c. walnuts
1/2 c. water
1/4 c. white rice, cooked
1 T. Mock Chicken Seasoning #2 (see p. 119)
1/4 + 1/8 t. garlic salt

Put in jar and refrigerate.

TOFU SPREAD

In Cuisinart or food processor:

1-1/4 c. tofu, firm crumbled (about 1 cube)
1 T. parsley flakes, or to taste
1 clove garlic, minced
1/4 t. salt
1/4 t. onion salt
2 T. water
1 t. lemon juice
or **1 T. lemon juice, for a sour cream spread**

Whiz in Cuisinart. Store in jar and serve as a bread spread.

Thanks Odette Boily for sharing recipe!

ALMOND BUTTER

Blend until creamy in Osterizer Mini-Blend jar or 1/2 pint canning jar:

1/2 c. almonds, raw, blanched
1/2 c. water
1 t. honey, liquid
1/8 t. salt

Refrigerate. Keeps about 2 days.

WHIPPED PEANUT BUTTER

Blend until creamy in Osterizer Mini-Blend jar or 1/2 pint canning jar:

- **1/3 c. peanut butter**
- **1/3 c. water**
- **1/8 t. salt,** if peanut butter is unsalted

Refrigerate. Keeps about 2 days.

MIXED NUT SPREAD

Toast in oven for 10 minutes at 300° F.:

- **1/8 c. Brazil nuts, raw, chopped**
- **1/8 c. cashews, raw**
- **1/8 c. almonds, raw, blanched**
- **1/8 c. walnuts, raw**

Blend in blender until creamy in Osterizer Mini-Blend jar or 1/2 pint canning jar:

- **mixed nuts, toasted**
- **1/8 t. salt**
- **5 T. water**

Refrigerate. Keeps about 2 days.

APPLE DATE SPREAD

Boil gently all ingredients together until soft and the consistency of jam. Add more juice if necessary.

- **2 c. apples, finely chopped** *or* **grated**
- **2 c. dates, chopped small**
- **3/4 c. apple juice**
- **pinch of salt**

Optional: **1 c. pineapple, unsweetened and crushed**

TAHINI SPREAD

Blend and mash:

2 c. garbanzos (chick peas), cooked and drained (1–19 oz. can)
3 T. tahini (unhulled sesame seed butter)
1 t. garlic salt
4 T. Soy Mayonnaise (see p. 83) **or to taste**

Fold in:

2–4 T. Spanish onion, chopped or to taste
1/4 c. celery, chopped very fine

Serve with lettuce.

Thank you Carole Minnick for sharing recipe!

APPLE BUTTER

Make thick applesauce using apple juice to cook sweet ripe apples to equal 3 cups of applesauce. Place applesauce in saucepan and cook until thick with:

3/4 c. dates, chopped

Simmer, stirring frequently until desired consistency or bake in 300° F. oven until thick.

A Pyrex dish works well for thickening the apple butter in the oven.

Note: Spy apples make delicious apple butter.

APRICOT JAM (yields about 2 pints)

Cut up in small pieces:

2 c. dried apricots

Put cut-up, dried apricots in small pot.

Add: **2-3/4 c. pineapple juice**

Bring to boil, then lower to lowest heat for 5 minutes.

continued...

Add: **1/3 c. dehydrated apples,**
made into powder in coffee grinder*
1/2 c. dehydrated pineapples,
made into powder in coffee grinder**
pinch of salt

Continue to simmer for 20 minutes, stirring occasionally.
* Measure dehydrated apples after grinding.
** Measure dehydrated pineapple before grinding.

DRIED FRUIT MARMALADE

Place in saucepan and simmer approximately 20 minutes, stirring frequently until thick:

1 c. dried apricots,
cut in small pieces
1 c. pineapple, unsweetened, crushed and well drained
1/2 c. Sultana raisins,
cut in small pieces
3/4 c. dates,
cut in small pieces
1-1/4 c. pineapple juice, unsweetened
1 T. orange juice, frozen, thawed from concentrate

Cool. Place in containers and refrigerate or freeze. Keeps at least 2 weeks in refrigerator.

STRAWBERRY JAM

In pot: **2 c. strawberries, frozen then thawed**

Use Mini-blender—Blend dry and measure after blending:

2/3 c. dried apples
1/2 c. dried pineapple

Combine dried fruit granules and frozen strawberries and a pinch of salt.

Bring to boil, then simmer on lowest temperature on stove for 20 minutes till jam is thick. Stir occasionally.

Store in refrigerator when cool.
It's delicious!

GRAPE JAM

Bring to boil, then let stand to cool:

1-1/2 c. grape juice, unsweetened
1 c. raisins

Blend above mixture 1 minute, then add and blend:

2 T. arrowroot powder

Cook until thick. Cool, place in container and refrigerate.

PLUM JAM

Wash, pit, chop in blender and set aside:

2 c. plums, purple , soft and ripe

Blend:

1/3 c. dried prunes, soft and chopped
(if prunes are very firm, soak overnight or until soft)
1/3 c. water

Place above mixtures in saucepan and add:

3/4 c. dates, chopped

Cook, stirring frequently—10 minutes. Store in jars or freeze.

TIPS ON SANDWICH MAKING

1. Vary breads.
2. Spreads—right to the edges.
3. Sprouts may be put in a separate container to add to sandwiches when eaten (or lettuce, etc.).
4. Be generous with fillings.
5. Cut bread in half or squares and wrap securely.

SANDWICH FILLINGS

1. Whipped peanut butter (see p. 173) with washed raisins.
2. Whipped peanut butter with banana slices or honey.
3. Soy Mayonnaise (see p. 83) and dates.
4. Mashed beans with finely chopped celery, green onions or with olives and Soy Mayonnaise.
5. Tomato sandwich.
6. Sliced cucumber with Cashew Pimento Cheese Spread (see p. 167).
7. Burgers.
8. Cold entrées mashed with Soy Mayonnaise.
9. Mockzarella sandwich.
10. Cashew Pimento Cheese with olives.
11. Tasty Mexicalli Loaf (see p. 34) with black chopped olives.

GRILLED CASHEW PIMENTO CHEESE SANDWICH

Spread sliced bread generously with Cashew Pimento Cheese Spread (see p. 167) and make into a sandwich.

On a Silverstone frying pan, brush lightly with olive oil. Grill sandwich to golden.
Delicious with soups or stews!

HOMMUS TAHINI

Blend: **1/2 c. tahini** (unhulled sesame seed butter)
1 clove garlic, crushed
or **garlic powder** (or garlic salt and omit salt)
2 c. garbanzos (chick peas), mashed, cooked and lightly-salted
salt to taste
2 T. lemon juice

Store in the refrigerator.

FALAFELS FOR PITA BREAD

Mix well in large bowl:

- **1 c. water**
- **1/2 c. parsley, chopped**
- **1 t. salt**
- **1/2 T. onion powder**
- **1/2 T. honey, liquid**
- **1-1/2 t. cumin**
- **2 t. basil**
- **1/2 t. coriander**
- **1 t. lemon juice**
- **1 t. Maggi (see p. 2)**
- **1 t. garlic powder**
- **1/2 t. garlic salt**
- **1 c. millet, cooked**
- **1/2 c. garbanzos (chick peas), cooked and mashed**
- **1 c. bread crumbs, whole wheat, toasted**
  or **zwieback crumbs**
- **1/2 c. Brazil nuts, ground fine**
- **1/2 c. sunflower seeds, ground fine**
- **2 T. tahini** (unhulled sesame seed butter)

Form into balls or patties and bake on Silverstone cookie sheet 30 to 40 minutes or on Silverstone frying pan with a trickle of oil until golden.

Note: Instead of zwieback crumbs, you may use "Finn" crisp, crunchy, thin, rye bread crumbs.

TOFU-KETCHUP SANDWICH

- **1-1/4 c. tofu**
- **1/2 t. onion salt**
- **2-1/2 t. Mock Chicken Seasoning #2 (see p. 119)**
- **2 t. Ketchup (see p. 82), or to taste**

Lightly mayonnaise bread.
Spread on filling.

Optional: Olives or green pepper

OPEN-FACED SANDWICHES

On slice of toast:

slices of Sunflower Seed Loaf (see p. 26), heated
or **Tofu Pecan Loaf (see p. 16)**

Pour Brown Gravy over the above.

or On slice of toast:

Cashew Loaf (see p. 14)
or **nut loaf of choice**
"Chick" Gravy (see p. 65)
or **Chicken-Like Gravy (see p. 66)**
or **Garbanzo Gravy (see p. 66)**

Serve as entrée.

PARTY CHEEZE BUNS

Sauté in 1 t. oil and 1 T. water:

1/2 c. green pepper, chopped fine
1/8 t. salt

When barely done, put in bowl.

Add: **1 c. tofu, crumbled**
1/2 t. onion salt
1/2 c. Cashew Pimento Cheese Sauce (see p. 65)
2 T. Ketchup (see p. 82)
1/4 c. black olives *or* **green olives, chopped**

Mix lightly.

Cut buns in half and spread generously with filling.

Take a little bread out of bun if you want them to fit together. Wrap in foil and heat when ready to serve or, if you like crusty buns, just heat on a cookie sheet and serve.

Serve with a nice fruit salad.

PIZZA

Use favorite bread recipe.
Roll dough as thin as possible. Put on greased pizza pan or cookie sheet. Let rise about 10 minutes. Bake at 350° F. for 20 minutes. Cool on rack.

Store in covered container or airtight bag till next day.
The next day, add:

Pizza Sauce (see p. 180)
Cashew Pimento Cheese (see p. 65)
green pepper, chopped or sliced
olives, black and sliced
pineapple chunks, drained
(or whatever— your choice!)

Suggestion: Pizza buns for mini pizzas—Large, whole wheat buns sliced in half; put toppings on; heat in oven and serve.

PIZZA SAUCE

Sauté in pot:

1 T. oil
1/2 c. green pepper, chopped very fine
1/8 t. salt

Add: **1 T. water,** if needed

Add and simmer:

4 c. tomatoes, canned
1/4 t. oregano
3/4 t. sweet basil
1 t. garlic powder
1/2 c. tomato paste
1 t. honey, liquid, (if tomatoes are tart—add honey to taste)
3/4 t. onion salt

Thicken with **1 T. arrowroot powder** (or cornstarch) **in 2** *or* **3 T. water** to dissolve.

Thought for the day

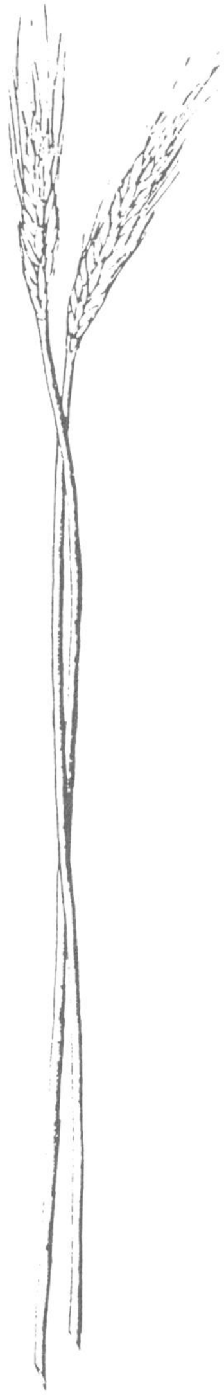

Spreads, jams and sandwich fillings can be prepared, or made special for someone you love.

Mary's beautiful act of love in the story of the alabaster box in the Bible, adds a new dimension to all we do, for her only motive was unselfish love. Mary loved Jesus; in Him she had found mercy, forgiveness and grace, and her heart was filled with real heart appreciation. She heard Him speak of His approaching death and in her deep love and sorrow she longed to honor Him. Extravagantly she spent her all to buy an alabaster box of special perfume to anoint His body. Then she heard He might be crowned King.

Quietly Mary slipped in where Jesus was a guest at a meal and broke the alabaster box of fragrant perfume, pouring it on His head and His feet. Weeping she knelt at His feet kissing them, and wiping them with her long flowing hair. They were tears of repentant love and deep gratitude. Her unselfish love and sacrifice was an unconscious expression to the world of the spirit of Jesus' love and His great sacrifice. It was an illumination of the special meaning of the truth of the cross. It meant so much to Jesus, a loving memory He took with Him to Calvary. He saw in Mary's motive the true reflection of His great love for us.

Remember, God loves you with an infinite love, too.

Notes

Desserts

REMEMBER!

"The more we depend upon the fresh fruit just as it is plucked from the tree, the greater will be the blessing." *Counsels on Diet and Foods, p. 309.*

FRUIT SALAD COMBINATIONS

A FAVORITE FRUIT SALAD

about 2 c. fresh or frozen strawberries
1 small can unsweetened pineapple dessert bits
3 or 4 oranges, cut up or in sections
3 sliced bananas

Optional: 1/2 c. Thompson (green) seedless grapes

AMBROSIA

Orange sections rolled in shredded, super fine, unsweetened coconut and drained, unsweetened pineapple chunks, pecan halves and seedless green grapes.

BANANAS AND FRUIT

In sherbet dish:	sliced bananas
Trickle over them:	undiluted frozen pineapple or orange juice (thawed)
Add:	green grapes, strawberries, pineapple chunks, or desired fruit

PEARS and BLUEBERRIES

In fruit nappe:	2 halves of canned pears, sliced lengthwise

Fill pear bowl with fresh blueberries.

FRUIT BANANA SPLIT

1 wedge honeydew melon—to resemble banana split boat
1/2 peach, rounded side up
top with 1/2 red cherry
bunch of grapes—draped over edge of honeydew

PAPAYA DELIGHT

1/2 papaya—sliced lengthwise (scoop out seeds)

Add: pineapple chunks, seedless green grapes,
strawberries

RASPBERRY DELIGHT

In a sherbet dish: fresh raspberries
a few pecan pieces
1 t. undiluted, frozen pineapple juice
or frozen orange juice (thawed)

Other suggested fruit with above recipe—blueberries.

LE PARFAIT "PARFAIT"

watermelon balls
honeydew melon balls
or canary melon balls

Optional: Add fresh blueberries or green Thompson seedless grapes topped with a strawberry and a sprig of mint.

ORANGE FRUIT CUP OR BASKET

(WITH FRESH FRUIT INSIDE)

For fruit cup—cut an orange in half and remove orange segments to leave just the half orange peel.

For fruit basket—leave a 1" wide strip from the top half of orange as a "handle" attached to the bottom orange cup.

Fill the cup or basket with:

orange sections, unsweetened pineapple tidbits,
whole fresh strawberries and raspberries, and
green Thompson seedless grapes

MELON DELIGHT

Peel and slice honeydew melon in about 1" thick rings. Garnish side with a little mint.

The center can be filled with strawberries, any berries or grapes, a combination of melon balls, or fruit of choice.

CANDLELIGHT DESSERT—Individual Dessert

pineapple ring base with slices of mandarin orange around it

half a peeled banana for "candle"
a trickle of Almond Butter (see p. 172) for "wax"
top with red cherry "flame"
half a slice of orange or pineapple for "handle"
garnish with sprig of mint

FRUIT PARFAIT

layer of strawberries on the bottom
layer of canned or fresh peaches
layer of sliced bananas
or desired fruit layers
top with a little unsweetened shredded coconut, chopped pecans and cherry on top

DESSERT IDEAS

Stuffed Dates
Stuff moist, pitted date with half a walnut or pecan.

Stuffed Figs
Cut fig in half and stuff with walnut.

Bowl of dried fruits, nuts and seeds
e.g. raisins and almonds pumpkin, or sunflower seeds with raisins

Try a peanut butter and honey sandwich!

or

Tahini and honey on "Rye Krisp".

BAKED APPLES

Wash apples. Scoop out center core and seeds, but not going through to the bottom.

Add 1 t. frozen, unsweetened apple juice (undiluted) to each apple center.

Wash Sultana raisins, and stuff to top of apple.

continued...

For 3–4 apples in small casserole dish—add on bottom of casserole to set apples in:

1/2 c. apple juice, frozen and unsweetened (undiluted)

If larger casserole, add more apples—use above proportions. Cover casserole. Bake 25–35 minutes depending on apple variety and size of apples.

When serving, use juice remaining in casserole and pour over apple. They are nice just warm.

BANANA NUT LOG

2 bananas, peeled, on wax paper

Cut each banana in half crosswise.
Put half banana on popsicle stick.
Cover each banana with Date Butter*.
Roll the bananas in chopped nuts.
Keep in refrigerator until ready to serve.

***Date Butter**
Simmer until soft:

1 c. dates, chopped
1/2 c. water
1/4 t. vanilla

Mash until smooth.

CAROB PEAR HELENE

Heat canned pears in Pyrex dish in oven (not too long or pears will be too soft and may fall apart). Just heat at 350° F. for 15–20 minutes.

Put desired amount of heated pears (drained) in individual dessert fruit nappes or sherbet dishes.

Pour over each dessert:

1 *or* **2 T. Carob Fudge Sauce** (see p. 188)

Top with chopped pecans and a cherry
or just heat toppingor serve cold!

CAROB FUDGE SAUCE

Makes 6 tablespoons.
In small bowl:

4 t.	**dark carob powder**
6 T.	**"Loma Linda Soyagen" powder**
3 T. + 1 t.	**honey, liquid (light)**
pinch of	**salt**
3 T.	**water**
1 t.	**vanilla**

Mix well. Put in jar. Refrigerate until ready to use.

GRAPE PEAR JELL

Soak 5 minutes in small pot:

2 T. (level)	**agar agar flakes (see p. 1)**
1 c.	**grape juice, unsweetened**
	or **homemade grape juice**

In small bowl, cut 2 c. drained, canned pears in small cubes.
Bring grape juice mixture in pot to boil—stirring constantly.
Simmer 1 minute to dissolve agar agar flakes.
Add additional 1-1/2 c. unsweetened grape juice.
Mix well and pour over pears in bowl.
Refrigerate.
Serve plain or with Creamy Pear Topping (see p. 200).

PRUNE PLUMS

Select and wash 1 pint of nice, plump prunes.
Add 1 quart of water.
Set in refrigerator—48 hours.

They will be just like plump, delicious plums.

STUFFED PRUNES

Stuff with toasted almonds

or

Pit the prunes by cutting a slit along the side of each prune and replacing the stone with a teaspoon of whipped Almond Butter (see p. 172) and garnish with a red cherry.

PINEAPPLE PUDDING

Blend in blender:

2 c.	**millet, cooked** (cook according to directions)
1-1/3 c.	**pineapple juice, unsweetened**
pinch of	**salt**
3 T.	**honey, liquid**
1 t.	**vanilla**

Remove from blender and fold in:

3/4 c.	**pineapple, unsweetened and crushed**
1/4 c.	**coconut, unsweetened and shredded**

Pour in sherbet dishes.
When ready to eat, garnish with a little coconut on top and a cherry or berry.

LEMON COCONUT CREAM

Serve as cream over Delicious Fruit Sauce (see p. 190).
Blend in blender till creamy (1 minute):

1 c.	**water, boiling**
1/2 c.	**coconut, unsweetened and shredded**

Add and blend (if too thick, add more pineapple juice):

1–14 oz. can	**pineapple tidbits, "Del Monte" unsweetened**
1/4 t.	**salt**
1/2 t.	**lemon extract**
1/2 c.	**"Loma Linda Soyagen"***

Refrigerate.
*Use kind which contains corn syrup.

DELICIOUS FRUIT SAUCE

Make about 1 quart of applesauce. Pare apples, simmer in apple juice instead of water. Add a pinch of salt.

Set aside and let cool.

Wash, core and dice 6 sweet apples in about 3/4" cubes, leaving skin on. Simmer in pineapple juice which has been drained from 1–14 oz. can of unsweetened pineapple tidbits. Add more pineapple juice while cooking, if needed.

Add:

1/4 c. dried apricots, cut in strips
3/4 c. raisins

Simmer about 10 minutes or until the apples are almost done—not mushy. Remove from heat.

Add:

1–14 oz. can pineapple tidbits, drained (cut tidbits in half)

Fold in quart of applesauce. Let cool. It is sweeter when cool. Add sliced bananas. Serve as a dessert with Lemon Coconut Cream (see p. 189) or as hot sauce over cereal in the morning with Lemon Coconut Cream.

APRICOT CANDY

Combine in large bowl and mix well:

3/4 c. dried apricots, ground
3/4 c. pecans, ground
1/3 c. coconut, unsweetened and shredded
1 t. lemonade, frozen and undiluted
1 t. orange juice, frozen and undiluted

If still too dry, add sufficient orange juice to be able to roll candy in unsweetened shredded coconut.

Faith in God is essential for health. In order to have perfect health, our hearts must be filled with love and hope and joy in the Lord. My Life Today, p. 149.

DATE "BON BONS"

Simmer together until soft, then cool:

2 c. dates, chopped
1/2 c. orange juice

Put in large bowl and add:

1 c. walnuts, chopped fine
1-1/2 c. coconut, unsweetened and shredded
1/2 t. vanilla

Mix well and roll in unsweetened shredded coconut.
Refrigerate "bon bons".

Thanks Joan Barker for sharing recipe!

TROPICANA FRUIT BALLS

Grind and put in a large bowl:

1 c. figs
1 c. dates, pitted
2 c. raisins, washed and drained
1 c. dried apricots

Add: **1 c. walnuts, chopped coarsely**

To moisten, add equal amounts of lemon juice and honey. Mix well. Shape into little round balls.
Roll in unsweetened shredded coconut.
Put in container and store in refrigerator.

The dessert should be placed on the table and served with the rest of the food; for often, after the stomach has been given all it should have, the dessert is brought on, and it is just that much too much. Counsels on Diet and Foods, *p.334.*

PINEAPPLE TOFU CHEESECAKE

CRUMB MIXTURE FOR BASE
Use 6-1/2" x 8" *or* 8" x 8" Pyrex dish.
Mix well in bowl:

1/2 c. granola (see p. 142), ground in blender
1 t. oil
1 T. water

For thicker crumb base use:

1 c. granola, ground in blender
1 T. oil
2 T. water

Pat down firmly with hands to cover bottom of the Pyrex dish. Bake at 350° F. for 10 minutes for first crumb base, or until golden for thicker crumb base.

PINEAPPLE FILLING (to pour over crumb base)
Soak and set aside for 5 minutes:

2 T. agar agar flakes (see p. 1)
1/2 c. water, cold

Blend in blender till creamy (1 minute):

1/2 c. pineapple juice
1/2 c. cashews, raw, washed

Add and blend until creamy:

3/4 c. pineapple dessert bits, drained and unsweetened
or **pineapple chunks**
1/4 t. salt
1/4 c. + 1 T. honey, liquid (light)
1/2 t. lemon extract
1/2 t. lemon rind, grated

Drain and crumble:

10 oz. tofu, firm

Bring agar agar flakes and water to a rolling boil and add to blender ingredients. Add crumbled tofu. Blend quickly as it sets fast. Pour over crumb base to set.
Chill in the refrigerator.

continued...

Just before serving, cut in squares and cover with pineapple topping (thickened, crushed pineapple—sweetened to taste) or cherry pie filling or topping of choice!

"YUMMY" FRUIT CAKE

In large bowl:

2 c. dates, chopped
1/2 lb. dried pineapple, honey-dipped, chopped fine
(purchase from health food store–about 1 1/2 cups)
1-1/4 c. walnuts, chopped
1 c. pecans
1-3/4 c. coconut, unsweetened and fine shredded
1 c. currants

Blend in blender until creamy, then add to above mixture:

2/3 c. almonds, raw, blanched
3/4 c. water
1/8 t. salt
1 t. vanilla
1 T. arrowroot powder

Lastly add: **1/4 c. honey, liquid**

Mix all together, and mix well.
Pack very firmly in 3 little cake pans 5-1/2" x 3" x 2-1/4" deep, that have been greased and lined with wax paper and greased again.

Bake at 300° F. for 50 minutes or until top is lightly golden. Allow to cool completely before removing from pans. Refrigerate. Slice with a sharp knife while chilled.

The home should be to the children the most attractive place in the world and the mother's presence should be its greatest attraction. By gentle discipline, in loving words and acts, mothers may bind the children to their hearts. The Faith I Live By, p. 264.

DELECTABLE STRAWBERRY PIE

Prepare Almond Pie Shell (see p. 196)

FILLING:

Wash and drain 3 pints Fresh Strwberries.

GLAZE AND BINDER:

7 lg. strawberries, ripe
5 soft dates, pitted
1 banana
1 T. lemon juice, fresh

Fold in 2 pints of strawberries in above glaze.
Pour in Almond Pie Shell (see p. 196).
Decorate top with 1 pint of strawberries cut in half lengthwise.
Refrigerate before serving at least 1 hour.

Thanks Kay Chamberlain for sharing recipe!

DATE NUT CHEWS

Heat in pan:

1 c. date pieces, soft
1/2 c. pecans, chopped
drizzel honey over to stick together

Drop on cookie sheets with wooden spoon.
Bake at 300° for 15–20 minutes.

Thanks Eriann Hullquist for sharing recipe!

SPECIAL OCCASIONS FRESH FRUIT CAKE

See picture on back of cookbook.

Use a round watermelon and slice the two ends off horizontally, leaving the center section at least 3" or 4" thick.

Mark the sides of this section in patterns to put the fresh fruits on the outside skin with toothpicks, i.e. raspberries, grapes, strawberries, blueberries, slices of nectarines, or apples or any fruit in season that you can work with.

Top with a swirl or spiral of honeydew slices, cantaloupe, watermelon, etc. (maybe alternating).

SPECIAL OCCASIONS:

For birthdays—candles and fresh flowers in the center on top
For children—plastic animals, etc.
For babies—stork, plastic carriage
For bridal showers—bride and groom

Be creative—for better health!

WHOLE WHEAT PASTRY PIE CRUST

Mix well in bowl:

1-1/2 c. flour, pastry, whole wheat, stone-ground (soft wheat)
1/2 t. salt

Emulsify with a fork:

1/2 c. corn oil, "Mazola", chilled
1/3 c. water, cold

Mix only until blended, then use hands to press dough together. Divide in half and form a round pat. Then flatten and roll gently between wax paper to size of pie plate. If bottom layer wrinkles, turn over, remove and use a new piece of wax paper on top.

Remove top layer of wax paper and center the dough side in pie plate. Remove wax paper gently from center out. Flute and prick with fork for single baked shell or leave whole for unbaked shells (when putting on a top with filling to bake).

Bake at 425° F. for 8–10 minutes or until golden.

ALMOND PIE SHELL

Makes 1 Large and 1 small pie shells.
(Tastes like Graham cracker pie shell.)

In food processor grind till fine:

2 c. almonds

Add and blend well:

1 c. dates, soft
1/8 t. salt
1/2 t. vanilla

Press thinly, yet firmly, into a pie plate with hands to shape shell.

COCONUT PASTRY

Mix in pie plate:

2 c. coconut, unsweetened and shredded

Emulsify and add:

4 T. oil
4 T. honey, liquid

Mix and press down with paper to shape of large pie plate. Bake at 325° F. for 5–8 minutes and watch closely. Cool. Special crust for Apple Raisin Pie filling.

APPLE RAISIN PIE

Boil on medium-low heat, stirring frequently until apples are tender:

2 c. raisins, washed
6 c. apples, chopped
1-1/8 c. dates, chopped
pinch of salt
2 c. apple juice

Mix: **1 T. arrowroot powder** with **1 T. water**
Add to fruit and cook until thick.
Cool and pour into baked pie shell.

RAISIN PIE

Simmer until raisins are plump:

1-1/2 c. Sultana raisins, washed
1-1/2 c. apple juice

Blend in blender until smooth (1 minute):

2/3 c. additional apple juice
2/3 c. additional raisins, washed
1 t. lemon juice
3 T. cornstarch

Combine both mixtures and cook until thick. Cool and pour into baked pie shell.

CAROB CHIFFON PIE

Soak in cold water for 5 minutes in small pot:

3 T. agar agar flakes (see p. 1)
3/4 c. water, cold

Blend in blender until creamy (1 minute):

1 c. cashews, raw
1 c. water

Add and blend:

1-1/2 c. soymilk ("Loma Linda Soyagen" with corn syrup)
2/3 c. honey, liquid
2 t. vanilla
1/2 t. salt
1/2 c. dark carob powder
1 t. "Caf-lib"
or **"Inka"**
(coffee substitute made from roasted grains)
1/3 c. "Loma Linda Soyagen" powder with corn syrup

Bring agar agar flakes to a rolling boil, stirring constantly. Add to blender and blend quickly. Pour in baked pie shell and set in refrigerator for about 2 hours.

PUMPKIN CHIFFON PIE

Soak and set aside for 5 minutes:

2 T. agar agar flakes **(see p. 1)**
1/2 c. water

Combine in saucepan and cook until soft, then set aside to cool:

1-3/4 c. dates, chopped
3/4 c. water

Blend in blender until creamy (1 minute):

1/2 c. cashews, raw
1/2 c. water

Blend cashew and date mixture, then add and blend:

14 oz. pumpkin, unsalted and mashed
If using canned thick pumpkin add 1/4 c. water to recipe
1/2 t. salt
2 T. honey or to taste
1/2 t. vanilla flavoring
1/2 t. orange extract
2 t. corriander, ground

Bring the agar agar flakes and water to a rolling boil . Combine mixtures and blend, using spatula to pull the mixture from sides to center in blender. Be patient as mixture is very thick. When creamy, pour into Almond Pie Shell (see p. 196) and chill. (If you have a food processor, use it to mix ingredients.)

BANANA CREAM PIE

Blend in blender until creamy (1 minute):

1/2 c. cashews, raw
1 c. water
1 c. dates, chopped
1 t. vanilla
pinch of salt
2 T. arrowroot powder

Add and blend for 1 minute: **additional 1 c. water**

Pour into saucepan. Cook, stirring constantly until thick—may take 8–10 minutes. Cool. In 8" baked pie shell, layer half of cream filling, then layer of sliced bananas, then remainder of filling. Top with coconut, fresh strawberries or cherries.

BANANA CREAM PARFAIT

In sherbet dishes, place alternate layers of Banana Cream Pie Filling (see p. 198) and sliced bananas. Top with coconut and chopped nuts. Place cherry on top.

BUTTER TARTS

Simmer in pot until fruit is plump, all the following ingredients:

2-1/2 c. water
2 c. Sultana raisins, washed
2 c. currants
2/3 c. honey, liquid
1 T. vanilla
1/8 t. almond extract
1/8 t. salt
1 T. lemon juice, fresh

Combine:

1 T. arrowroot powder
1/4 c. water, cold

Add to boiling mixture. Cook until clear.
Make pastry tart shells. Bake at 400° F. for 7 minutes. Fill hot, partially baked pastry shells with above filling. Turn oven to 375° F. Finish baking butter tarts 15–20 minutes in 375° F. oven. Remove from tart pans or muffin tins immediately. Cool on rack.

Note: the above is a big recipe. You might want to cut the filling recipe in half for a small family or, if not, they freeze beautifully.

Thanks Joan Barker for sharing recipe!

STRAWBERRY TARTS

Make sugarless Strawberry Jam (see p. 175). Fold in desired amount of fresh, sliced, sweet strawberries. Just before serving, top with Creme d'Soy Topping (see p. 200) and a whole strawberry.

CREME d'SOY TOPPING

Blend in blender until creamy (1 minute):

1/2 c. almonds, blanched
1/2 c. water

Add and blend:

1/2 c. water
1/8 t. salt
1/2 t. pure vanilla
2 T. honey, liquid (light)
1/2 c. Creme d'Soy powdered soy based creamer*

Continue blending, adding (1 t. at a time) Creme d'Soy powder until very thick.

Remove from blender and put in bowl.
Add 1 T. fresh lemon juice.
Mix well. Put in container and refrigerate.

*"Millers Solait Creme d'Soy" powdered soy based creamer.

CREAMY PEAR TOPPING

Blend until creamy (1 minute):

1/4 c. almonds, blanched
1/4 c. cashews, raw
1/2 c. water

Add:
1 c. pears, canned and drained
2 T. honey, liquid
1 t. vanilla
1/2 c. "Loma Linda Soyagen" (with corn syrup)

When the "Soyagen" is added, it will be very thick. Stir with fork and turn blender off and on until creamy and well-mixed.

Add **1 T. fresh lemon juice** and continue to turn blender off and on. Put in container and chill.
Delicious on tarts, as pudding topping and pies.

For best results use immediately!

APPLE CRISP

Wash, peel, core, and thinly slice **8 apples** or enough to fill a 7" x 11" x 2" deep Pyrex dish. Lightly grease Pyrex dish. Fill half full of sliced apples. Sprinkle **1/8 t. salt** over apples.
Mix **1 T. lemon juice with 2 T. water** and sprinkle evenly over apples. Wash **3/4 c. Sultana raisins** and spread evenly over apples. Add sufficient of the remaining sliced apples to go almost to the top of the Pyrex dish.

CRUMB TOPPING—in large bowl:

1/3 c. brown sugar
1/2 c. flour, pastry, whole wheat, stone-ground
1/4 t. salt
1 c. oats, quick
1/3 c. oil

Mix well by tumbling through fingers.
Optional: **2/3 c. chopped pecans in crumb mixture,** *or* **nuts of choice,** *or* **sunflower seeds.**
Cover apples with crumb topping. Bake at 375° F. for 10 minutes. Then at 350° F. for 30–45 minutes (depending on kind of apples; MacIntosh takes the least time, Spy apples take longer).

PEACH CRISP

In 7"x11" Pyrex dish: fill half full with canned, drained peaches , cut into quarters.
Add: **1 c. Dried Fruit Marmalade (see p. 175)**
Mix in evenly with peaches.
CRUMB TOPPING—mix in bowl:

1/2 c. flour, pastry, whole wheat, stone-ground
1/4 t. salt
1-1/4 c. oats, quick
1/2 c. walnuts *or* **pecans, chopped**
1 T. cornmeal

In small bowl emulsify and add to crumbs, tossing lightly:

1/3 c. oil
2 –3 T honey, liquid

Cover peaches with crumb topping. Bake at 350° F. for 30–35 minutes until golden.

FIG SQUARES

Mix crumb mixture in large bowl:

2 c. oats, quick
2/3 c. flour, pastry, whole wheat, stone-ground
1/3 c. sesame seeds
1/3 c. brown sugar
1/4 t. salt

Emulsify and add to dry ingredients:

1/3 c. oil
1/3 c. water

Mix well. Press half of mixture on bottom of 8" x 8" pan or its equivalent. Spread on filling. Cover with balance of crumb mixture. Press down lightly. Bake at 350° F. for 30–35 minutes.

FIG FILLING FOR FIG SQUARES

Cook, cool and puree:

2 c. figs, cut up
1/2 c. water
1 t. lemon juice
1/4 t. salt

Thanks Stephanie Preston Diemert for sharing recipe!

PINEAPPLE-DATE SQUARES

Crumb mixture in a bowl:

2 c. oats, quick
1 c. oat flour
1 c. coconut, unsweetened and shredded
1/2 c. sunflower seeds, ground
1/2 t. salt

Emulsify and add to crumb mixture:

1/3 c. oil
3 T. honey, liquid
1/3 c. pineapple juice

Mix well, tumbling through fingers. Press half of the mixture into a 7–1/2"x11–1/2" Pyrex dish.

continued...

FILLING

Cook until thick:

1–19 oz. can pineapple, crushed
1/4 c. figs *or* **prunes, cut up**
1-3/4 c. dates, cut up

Place filling on crumb mixture evenly.

Cover with remaining crumbs and press lightly but firmly. Bake at 350° F. for 35 minutes.

RAISIN BARS

RAISIN FILLING

In pot:

1–1/2 c. Sultana raisins, washed
2/3 c. water
1 t. lemon juice

Bring to boil, then lower to lowest heat and simmer 10 minutes.

Add: **1/4 c. water** with **1 t. arrowroot powder**
1/2 t. vanilla

Cook till thickened, then remove from heat to cool while making crumb mixture (won't be extra thick and that's the way you want it).

CRUMB BASE

In large bowl, add:

2 c. oats, quick
1 c. oat flour
1/2 c. walnuts, coarsely ground
1/2 t. salt
1/2 c. coconut, unsweetened and shredded

Emulsify:

1/3 c. oil
2 T. honey, liquid
1/3 c. water

Add to crumb mixture. Mix well by tumbling through fingers. Wash hands and shake excess water off.

In 7" x 11" or 8" x 8" Pyrex dish, flatten one-half to two-thirds of the crumb mixture on the bottom and press down with your fingers. Spread filling evenly over crumb mixture. Pour remaining crumb mixture over filling evenly. Press firmly with hand.

Bake at 350° F. for 25–30 minutes or till golden. Cool before removing from pans.

ORANGE DATE RAISIN BARS (oil free)

Cook filling in small pot till fairly thick, about 10 minutes:

1 c. dates, chopped and packed
1-1/2 c. Sultana raisins, washed
1-1/4 c. pineapple juice
1 t. lemon juice
1/2 t. vanilla

Set aside to cool.
In blender, blend into flour:

1-1/2 c. millet seed

Note: Texture is different than bought millet flour.
In large bowl, add:

blended millet seed
1 c. walnuts, ground
1/2 t. salt
2/3 c. coconut, unsweetened and shredded
1 t. orange rind
2/3 c. orange juice

Mix well. Spread half of crumb mixture in a 7-1/2" x 12" (approximately) size Pyrex dish. Pat down firmly with hands. Sread filling evenly over crumb mixture. Cover filling evenly with remaining crumbs and pat down firmly. Bake at 350° F. for 35 minutes or until golden.
Thanks Catherine Poplawski for sharing recipe!

CAROB BROWNIES

In large bowl mix well:

2/3 c. honey, liquid
1/4 c. Almond Butter (see p. 172)
1/4 t. salt
1/4 c. oil
2 t. vanilla
1 T. lemon juice
1/4 c. soymilk
1/3 c. dark carob powder
2/3 c. flour, pastry, whole wheat, stone-ground
1/4 c. rice flour, white
2/3 c. walnuts *or* pecans, chopped

continued...

Pour into greased Silverstone cake pan or 6-1/2" x 8" Pyrex dish. Bake at 350° F. for 25 minutes or until toothpick comes out clean. Time depends on size of baking dish and whether it's a non-stick pan.

Cool, then frost with Carob Frosting.

GLAZE FOR BROWNIES (OR CAROB FROSTING)

Mix in small bowl:

1 t.	**dark carob powder**
2 T.	**"Loma Linda Soyagen" powder**
1 T.	**honey, liquid**
pinch of	**salt**
2-1/2 t.	**water**
1/2 t.	**vanilla**

Mix well.

CAROB MINT PUDDING

Blend until creamy (1 minute):

1/2 c.	**cashews, raw**
1/2 c.	**water**

Add and blend:

1 c.	**tofu, well drained** (about 1 cube)
3 T.	**carob powder**
1/8 t.	**peppermint extract**
3 T.	**honey, liquid**
pinch of	**salt**

Chill and serve.

Better than gold is a peaceful home,
Where all the fireside charities come;
The shrine of love and the heaven of life,
Hallowed by mother, or sister, or wife.
However humble the home may be,
Or tried with sorrows by heaven's decree,
The blessings that never were bought or sold,
And center there, are better than gold.

Anon.

BANANA DATE COOKIES

In bowl: **2 c. bananas, ripe mashed**

Add:
1 c. dates, chopped
1/2 c. walnuts, chopped
1/2 t. salt
1 t. vanilla
1 c. raisins
1/2 c. coconut, unsweetened and shredded
2 c. oats, quick

Mix well.
Drop by tablespoonfuls on Silverstone cookie sheet.
Bake at 350° F. for 25 minutes.

CAROB CHIP COOKIES

Blend in blender until creamy (1 minute):

1/3 c. almonds, unblanched and not roasted
1/2 c. water

Add almond cream to bowl and add:

1/3 c. oil
1 t. vanilla
1/3 c. brown sugar
1/4 t. salt
1 1/2 c. oats, quick
1/4 c. oat flour
1/2 c. carob chips
1/3 c. walnuts *or* **pecans, chopped**

Mix well and drop by tablespoonfuls and shape on ungreased Silverstone cookie sheet.

Flatten a little with a fork.
Bake in preheated oven at 350° F. for 25 minutes. Let cookies cool on cookie sheet placed on rack.

Pleasant words are as an honeycomb, sweet to the soul, and health to the bones. Proverbs 16:24.

CAROLE'S COOKIES

Stew in pot, blend and cool:

1/2 c. apricots, chopped
1/2 c. dates, chopped
1/2 c. orange juice *or* **water**

In large bowl, mix together:

1/2 c. oil
1/4 c. brown sugar

Add cooled, stewed fruit mixture.

Add:
1 c. flour, soft whole wheat
1/2 t. salt
3/4 c. oats, quick
1/2 c. wheat germ
1/2 c. bran
1/2 c. walnuts, chopped
1/2 c. coconut, unsweetened and shredded
1/3 c. Sultana raisins, washed

Mix all together. Form into balls and flatten with fork on ungreased Silverstone cookie sheet.

Bake at 350° F. for 10 to 15 minutes or till done.

Thanks Carole Minnick for sharing recipe!

COCONUT MACAROONS

Mix in large bowl:
1 c. carrots, grated
1 t. almond extract
1/4 c. water
1/2 c. honey, liquid

Add:
2 c. coconut, unsweetened and shredded
1/4 c. flour, pastry, whole wheat, stone-ground
1/4 c. soy flour
1/2 t. salt

Let stand 10 minutes. Drop by spoonfuls on ungreased Silverstone cookie sheet.

Bake at 325° F. for 30 minutes.

CRISPY OAT COOKIES

Blend in blender till creamy, 1 minute (use mini-blender if available):

1/3 c. almonds, unblanced and not roasted
1/2 c. water

Put almond cream in a bowl.
Add and mix well:

1/3 c. oil
1 t. vanilla
1/3 c. brown sugar
1/4 t. salt
1-1/2 c. oats, quick
1/4 c. oat flour
1/2 c. Sultana raisins, washed
1/4 c. currants, washed
1/3 c. walnuts *or* **pecans, chopped**

Mix well and drop by tablespoonfuls and shape on ungreased Silverstone cookie sheet. Flatten a little with fork. Bake at 350° F. for 25 minutes or till golden on bottom. Let cookies cool on cookie sheet placed on rack.

PEANUT BUTTER COOKIES

In large bowl, mix till creamy:

1/3 c. crunchy peanut butter
1/3 c. honey, liquid
1/3 c. oil
1/3 c. water, cold
1 t. vanilla
1/2 t. salt

Add: **2 + 1 T. c. oat flour**

Mix well and let stand 5 minutes. Roll in little balls the size of small walnuts. Flatten with fork. Bake on ungreased Silverstone cookie sheet at 350° F. for 8 to 10 minutes. (Watch carefully, they burn easily.) Bake just till golden brown underneath cookie. Cool on rack and store in container.

Note: They may seem soft when you take them out of oven, but will crisp later.

PEAR COOKIES

In large bowl:

1 c. pears, drained and mashed
1 c. dates, chopped
2/3 c. pear juice *or* apple juice
1/2 c. walnuts, chopped
1/2 t. salt
2-1/2 c. oats, quick
1/2 c. Sultana raisins, washed
1 t. vanilla

Mix well. Let stand 5 minutes for oats to absorb moisture. Shape cookies on ungreased Silverstone cookies sheet. Bake at 350° F. for 20 minutes or till bottom is golden brown.

Let cool on cookie sheet, then store in container.

Thanks Catherine Poplawski for sharing recipe!

APPLE COOKIES

Instead of mashed pears, use:

1 c. applesauce, thick and homemade

PINEAPPLE COOKIES

Place in bowl:

1/2 c. oil
1/4 c. brown sugar
2/3 c. pineapple, unsweetened, crushed and drained
1/2 t. vanilla
1 c. flour, pastry, whole wheat, stone-ground
1/2 t. salt (scant)
1 c. oats, quick
3/4 c. raisins, washed, drained and seedless

Mix well. Drop by spoonfuls on Silverstone cookie sheet. Bake at 350° F. for 25 to 30 minutes.

VANILLA PUDDING

Blend in blender until creamy (1 minute):

1/2 c.	**cashews, raw**
1 c.	**water**
1 c.	**dates, chopped**
1 t.	**vanilla**
pinch of	**salt**
2 T.	**arrowroot powder**

Add and blend for 1 minute: **additional 1 c. water**

Pour into saucepan. Cook, stirring constantly until thick—may take 8 to 10 minutes.

Cool.
Serve in pudding dishes.
Top with coconut.

RAISIN-RICE PUDDING

Combine and mix well:

2 c.	**brown rice, cooked**
2 c.	**soy milk**
1 t.	**vanilla**
3/4 c.	**raisins**
1/2 c.	**dates, chopped**
1/4 t.	**salt**

Put into a baking dish and bake, uncovered, at 350° F. about 45 minutes.

Serve warm or chilled.

SAVORY POPCORN

Instead of salt and butter—

Try: Engevita yeast (see p. 2) and onion salt while hot

CREAMY CAROB MINTS

In large bowl:

3/4 c. honey, liquid
1/3 c. dark carob powder
4 t. vanilla
2 drops peppermint oil
1 c. "Loma Linda Soyagen" powder
1/8 t. salt
1 c. walnuts, chopped

Stir together.
Shape in little balls (wet hands occasionally—bon bons roll better). Roll in unsweetened shredded coconut. Place in container and refrigerate.

Thanks Carole Minnick for sharing recipe!

CAROB MINT "BON BONS"

Simmer dates and water till soft:

1/2 c. water
1 c. dates, chopped

When soft, put in bowl and cool.

Add: **1/8 t. salt**
1/3 c. dark carob powder
1/2 c. coconut, unsweetened and shredded
3 T. honey, liquid
1 c. peanut butter, smooth
1/2 c. walnuts, chopped
1/4 t. peppermint extract

Shape into small "bon bons".
Roll in unsweetened shredded coconut.
Put in container and store in refrigerator.

SUNFLOWER SEED "BON BONS"

Place in bowl:

1 c. honey, liquid
1 T. vanilla
1/3 c. dark carob powder
1/8 t. salt
1/4 c. "Loma Linda Soyagen" powder
2 c. sunflower seeds, ground (not too fine)
1 c. coconut, unsweetened and shredded

Mix well. Wet hands and roll in small "bon bons" in fine, unsweetened shredded coconut. Place in covered container and refrigerate. Nicest after 24 hours.

Thanks Joan Barker for sharing recipe!

SESAME SEED SNAPS

Grease a 7" x 11–1/2" Pyrex dish.
Mix well together in a small bowl:

1/4 c. brown sugar
1/4 c. honey, liquid

Dextrinize (see p. 2) in a "cast iron" frying pan approximately 5 to 7 minutes:

3 c. sesame seeds

Add honey mixture, and mix well quickly.
Pour into greased pan (see above). Grease hands and pat down. Cut while soft as these harden quickly.

Grains, fruits, nuts, and vegetables constitute the diet chosen for us by our Creator. These foods, prepared in as simple and natural a manner as possible, are the most healthful and nourishing. They impart a strength, a power of endurance and a vigor of intellect, that are not afforded by a more complex and stimulating diet. Counsels on Diet and Foods, p. 81.

Beverages

CAFFEINE

Stimulant

Average Contents

*instant coffee (per cup)	30–120 mg.
*brewed coffee	40–180 mg.
*decaffeinated coffee	less than 5 mg.
*tea	10–80 mg.
*cocoa	less than 50 mg.
*cola drinks (per can)	20–45 mg.
compound headache, cold preparation (per tablet) (e.g. Frosst 222 and Ornex*)	15–65 mg.
*"stay-awake" pills	100–200 mg.

Short-term Effects

*increased alertness and sleeplessness
*spontaneous tremor of hands
*increased pulse rate and blood pressure, irregular heart beat in some individuals

Long-term Effects

*effects of heavy use (more than 8 average cups a day)

- caffeine dependence (withdrawal symptoms include irritability, restlessness, and headache)
- insomnia, anxiety, stomach and duodenal ulceration
- also heart disease, bladder cancer, and birth defects are suspected

Reprinted from brochure *Coffee, Tea and Me* and used with permission from Addiction Research Foundation, Toronto, Canada.

Kind, cheerful, encouraging words will prove more effective than the most healing medicines. These will bring courage to the heart of the desponding and discouraged, and the happiness and sunshine brought into the family by kind acts and encouraging words will repay the effort tenfold. My Life Today, p. 152.

FIG TEA

Cut dried, juicy, plump California or Calamyrna figs in fourths. Put on Silverstone cookie sheet.
Bake at 275° F. for 1-1/2 to 2 hours, stirring occasionally, till the figs are like charcoal pellets.

To make Fig Tea:

1 piece of roasted fig per cup of water

Bring to boil, lower heat and simmer till desired strength, approximately 3 to 5 minutes.

If the beverage is too strong, it is more like a coffee substitute. Add more water—a delicious tea!

SOYBEAN COFFEE

Sort, clean and wash—soybeans.

Roast soybeans in oven at 400° F. for 40 minutes, till they start cracking and turn golden or light brown.

Blend in blender (not too small).

In percolator:

1 t. per 1 cup
4 t. per 4 cups

Home should be a place where cheerfulness, courtesy, and love abide; and where these graces dwell, there will abide happiness and peace. *<u>My Life Today</u>, p. 152.*

Thought for the day

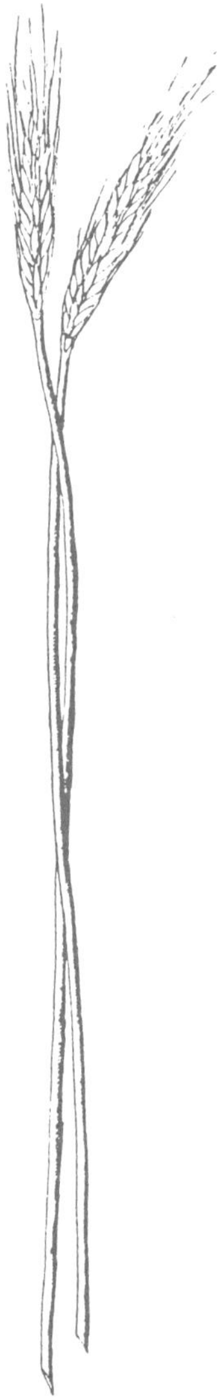

"I will praise thee; for I am fearfully and wonderfully made: marvellous are thy works; and that my soul knoweth right well." Psalm 139:14.

Praise God for the gift of sight, of hearing, of smelling, of tasting, of choosing. They are "gifts of love" from a wonderful Creator to His special creation. "Every good gift and every perfect gift is from above, and cometh down from the Father of lights,...." James 1:17.

Foods we choose, especially desserts, gift-wrapped by God are wholesome, nourishing and in perfect balance. Take the orange, high in fruit sugar, but it also contains proportionate amounts of nutrients needed in order to properly utilize those calories without depleting the body's vitamin and mineral store. The more we eat foods as given to us by God, the greater will be our blessing.

The One who made us, put the sweetness in the fruits for us to enjoy, the honey in the honeycomb for our delight. Then He adds, "It's not good to eat too much honey." Proverbs 25:27. What wisdom and love. How can we say "thank you" for such love and bring honor and glory to His name?

"What? know ye not that your body is the temple of the Holy Ghost which is in you, which ye have of God, and ye are not your own? For ye are bought with a price: therefore glorify God in your body, and in your spirit, which are God's."

I Corinthians 6:19, 20.

Remember, God loves you.

Notes

HOW MUCH GOD REALLY LOVES YOU

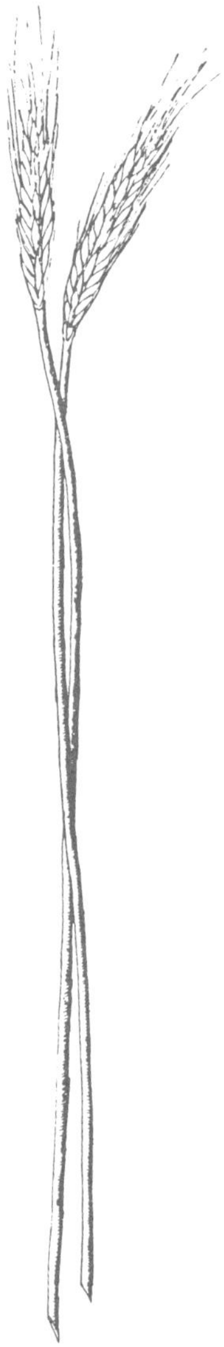

Throughout the "Thoughts for the Day" we have shared how much God loves you, now, may we share how much He really loves you.

Can you imagine how heartbroken God was when Adam and Eve ate of the forbidden fruit in the garden of Eden? (Genesis, ch.3) They were His special creation, created in His own image and they had chosen to listen to the enemy and disbelieve God.

Sorrow filled heaven—sorrow for Adam and Eve, and even greater sorrow when the angels heard how God's only Son, their beloved Commander, would go to earth and die in their place.

Can you imagine how Adam and Eve felt when they heard how much God really loved them? How Jesus had offered Himself, to take human nature, and by humiliation and sacrifice make a way of escape for them?

What wondrous love!

"...when Adam was assailed by the tempter, none of the effects of sin were upon him. He stood in the strength of perfect manhood, possessing the full vigor of mind and body. He was surrounded with the glories of Eden, and was in daily communion with heavenly beings. It was not thus with Jesus when He entered the wilderness to cope with Satan. For four thousand years the race had been decreasing in physical strength, in mental power, and in moral worth; and Christ took upon Him the infirmities of degenerate humanity. Only thus could He rescue man from the lowest depths of his degradation.

Many claim that it was impossible for Christ to be overcome by temptation. Then He could not have been placed in Adam's position; He could not have gained the victory that Adam failed to gain. If we have in any sense a more trying conflict than had Christ, then He would not be able to succor us. But our Saviour took humanity, with all its liabilities. He took the nature of man, with the possibility of yielding to temptation. We have nothing to bear which He has not endured.

At the birth of Jesus, Satan knew that One had come with a divine commission to dispute his dominion. He trembled at the angel's message attesting the authority of the newborn King. Satan well knew the position that Christ had held in heaven as the Beloved of the Father. That the Son of God should come to this earth as a man filled him with amazement and apprehension. He could not fathom the mystery of this great sacrifice. His selfish soul could not understand such love for the deceived race.

Not without hindrance was the Commander of heaven to win the souls of men to His kingdom. From the time when He was a babe in Bethlehem, He was continually assailed by the evil one... The forces of the confederacy of evil were set upon His track to engage in warfare against Him, and if possible to prevail over Him. At the Saviour's baptism, Satan was among the witnesses. He saw the Father's glory overshadowing His Son. He heard the voice of Jehovah testifying to the divinity of Jesus... Satan had hoped that God's abhorrence of evil would bring an eternal separation between heaven and earth, but "God so loved the world, that He gave His only begotten Son, that whosoever believeth in Him should not perish, but have everlasting life." *Desire of Ages*, pp. 115-117.

After Jesus' baptism, He was led by the Spirit into the wilderness. It was a dreary, barren, desolate place surrounded by wild beasts. Everything around was repulsive to Jesus. "He went to the wilderness to be alone, to contemplate His mission and work. By fasting and prayer He was to brace Himself for the bloodstained path He was to travel. How should He begin His work of freeing the captives held in torment by the destroyer?... When Jesus entered the wilderness He was shut in by the Father's glory. Absorbed in communion with God, He was lifted above human weakness. But the glory departed, and He was left to battle with temptation. It was pressing upon Him every moment. His human nature shrank from the conflict that awaited Him." *I Selected Messages*, p. 227.

Jesus tells us in John 8:28 "I do nothing of myself;" "For I came down from heaven, not to do mine own will, but the will of him that sent me." John 6:38. The "will" is "the choice."

"The Lord Jesus came to our world, not to reveal what a God could do, but what man could do, through faith in God's power to help in every emergency." *Ms. 1, 1892.*

"He felt the overwhelming tide of woe that deluged the world. He realized the strength of indulged appetite and unholy passion which controlled the world and had brought upon man inexpressible suffering.

In man's behalf He must show self-denial, perseverance, and firmness of principle... stronger than hunger or death." *Confrontation*, pp. 36-37.

"For forty days He ate and drank nothing.... The controlling power of depraved appetite, and the grievous sin of indulging it, can only be understood by the length of the fast which our Saviour endured that He might break its power." *God's Amazing Grace*, p. 164.

"The Saviour was faint from hunger, He was craving for food, when Satan came suddenly upon Him. Pointing to the stones which strewed the desert, and which had the appearance of loaves, the tempter said, "If thou be the Son of God, command that these stones be made bread." Though he appears as an angel of light, these first words betray his character. "If thou be the Son of God." Here is the insinuation of distrust. Should Jesus do what Satan suggests, it would be an acceptance of the doubt. The tempter plans to overthrow Christ by the same means that were so successful with the human race in the beginning. How artfully had Satan approached Eve in Eden!

Would God treat his own Son thus? Would He leave Him in the desert with wild beasts, without food,...without comfort? "...show Thy power by relieving Thyself of this pressing hunger. Command that this stone be made of bread."

Not without a struggle could Jesus listen in silence to the arch deceiver. But the Son of God was not to prove His divinity to Satan....Evidence would have been worthless to break the power of rebellion in his heart. And Christ was not to exercise divine power for His own benefit. He had come to bear trial as we must do, leaving us an example of faith and submission.

Christ said to the tempter, "Man shall not live by bread alone, but by every word that proceedeth out of the mouth of God."...In the wilderness, when all means of sustenance failed, God sent His people manna from heaven....This provision was to teach them that while they trusted in God and walked in His ways He would not forsake them. The Saviour now practiced the lesson He has taught to Israel. By the word of God, succor [help] had been given to the Hebrew host, and by the same word it would be given to Jesus....In the presence of the witnessing universe, He testified that it is a less calamity to suffer whatever may befall than to depart in any manner from the will of God.

Only by the word could He resist temptation. "It is written," He said. And unto us are given "exceeding great and precious promises; that by these ye might be partakers of the divine nature, having escaped the corruption that is in the world through lust." 2 Peter 1:4. Every promise in God's word is ours.... When assailed by temptation, look not to circumstances or to the weakness of self, but to the power of the word. All its strength is yours. "Thy word," says the Psalmist, "have I hid in mine heart that I might not sin against Thee." "By the word of Thy lips I have kept me from the paths of the destroyer." Psalm 119:11; Psalm 17:4." *Desire of Ages*, pp. 118, 119, 121, 123.

"Our Redeemer withstood the power of Satan upon this great leading temptation, which imperils the souls of men. If man should overcome this temptation, he could conquer on every other point." *God's Amazing Grace*, p. 164.

"Let him who is struggling against the power of appetite look to the Saviour in the wilderness of temptation. See Him in His agony upon the cross... He has endured all that it is possible for us to bear. His victory is ours. Jesus rested upon the wisdom and strength of His heavenly Father. He declares, "The Lord God will help Me; therefore shall I not be confounded....and I know that I shall not be ashamed....Behold, the Lord God will help Me." Isaiah 50:7-9" *Desire of Ages*, p. 123.

"Temptation is resisted when a man is powerfully influenced to do a wrong action, and knowing that he can do it, resists by faith, with a firm hold upon divine power. This was the ordeal through which Christ passed." *The Youth Instructor, July 20, 1899*

Not only in the wilderness but all through His life on earth Jesus suffered. "He...hath suffered being tempted." Hebrews 2:18. "Who in the days of His flesh offered up prayers and supplications with strong crying and tears unto Him that is able to save Him from death..." Hebrews 5:7.

"For we have not an high priest which cannot be touched with the feeling of our infirmities, but was in all points tempted like as we are, yet without sin.

Let us therefore come boldly unto the throne of grace, that we may obtain mercy, and find grace to help in time of need." Hebrews 4:15, 16.

"He gave all there was of Himself." *Review & Herald, April 4, 1912.*

Jesus acknowledged openly that He had as much of a conflict in His soul as I have in mine. He had two wills—two choices.

"In company with His disciples, the Saviour slowly made His way to the garden of Gethsemane. The Passover moon, broad and full, shone from a cloudless sky... As He neared Gethsemane, He became strangely silent... Throughout His life on earth He had walked in the light of God's presence....But now He seemed to be shut out from the light of God's sustaining presence. Now He was numbered with the transgressors. The guilt of fallen humanity He must bear. Upon Him who knew no sin must be laid the iniquity of us all. So dreadful does sin appear to Him, so great is the weight of guilt He must bear that He is tempted to fear it will shut Him out forever from His Father's love.... He exclaims, "My soul is exceeding sorrowful, even unto death."

The disciples had marked the change that came over their Master. Never before had they seen Him so utterly sad and silent. As He proceeded, this strange sadness deepened....His form swayed as if He were about to fall... Every step that He now took was labored effort. He groaned aloud, as if suffering under the pressure of a terrible burden. Twice His companions supported Him or He would have fallen to the earth.

Near the entrance to the garden, Jesus left all but three of the disciples, bidding them pray for themselves and for Him. With Peter, James, and John, He entered its secluded recesses....He desired them to spend the night with Him in prayer. Yet He could not bear that even they should witness the agony He was to endure.

"Tarry ye here," He said, "and watch with Me."

He went a little distance from them...and fell prostrate upon the ground. He felt that by sin He was being separated from His father. The gulf was so broad, so black, so deep, that His spirit shuddered before it....As man He must suffer the consequences of man's sin....

Terrible was the temptation to let the human race bear the consequences of its own guilt....If He could only know that His disciples understood and appreciated this He would be strengthened....He feared that in His human nature He would be unable to endure the coming conflict with the powers of darkness.

Behold Him contemplating the price to be paid for the human soul. In His agony He clings to the cold ground, as if to prevent Himself from being drawn farther from God. The chilling dew of night falls upon His prostrate form, but He heeds it not. From His pale lips comes the bitter cry, "O My Father, if it be possible, let this cup pass from Me." Yet even now He adds, "Nevertheless not as I will, but as Thou wilt."

The human heart longs for sympathy in suffering. This longing Christ felt to the very depths of His being. In the supreme agony of His soul He came to His disciples with a yearning desire to hear some words of comfort....He longed to know that they were praying for Him and for themselves.

Rising with painful effort, He staggered to the place where He had left His companions. But He "findeth them asleep."...The disciples awakened at the voice of Jesus, but they hardly knew Him. His face was so changed by anguish....He staggered back to the place of His former struggle. His suffering was even greater than before.... "His sweat was as it were great drops of blood falling down to the ground."

The fate of humanity trembled in the balance. Christ might even now refuse to drink the cup apportioned to guilty man. It was not yet too late. He might wipe the bloody sweat from His brow, and leave man to perish in his iniquity. He might say, let the transgressor receive the penalty of his sin, and I will go back to My Father. Will the Son of God drink the bitter cup of humiliation and agony?....The words fall tremblingly from the pale lips of Jesus, "O My Father, if this cup may not pass away from Me, except I drink it, Thy will be done."

Three times he has uttered that prayer. Three times has humanity shrunk from the last, crowning sacrifice. But now the history of the human race comes up before the world's Redeemer. He sees that the transgressors of the law, if left to themselves must perish. He sees the helplessness of man. He sees the power of sin. The woes and lamentations of a doomed world rise before Him. He beholds its impending fate, and His decision is made. He will save man at any cost to Himself. He accepts His baptism of blood, that through Him perishing millions may gain everlasting life... He will not turn from His mission.... Having made the decision, He fell dying to the ground.... God suffered with His Son....There was silence in heaven....

No way for escape was found for the Son of God. In this awful crisis, when everything was at stake, when the mysterious cup trembled in the hand of the sufferer, the heavens opened, a light shone forth,...and the almighty angel who stands in God's presence occupying the position from which Satan fell, came to the side of Christ. The angel came not to take the cup from Christ's hand, but to strengthen Him to drink it, with the assurance of the Father's love. He came to give power to the divine-human suppliant. He pointed Him to the open heavens, telling Him of the souls that would be saved as the result of His sufferings....He told Him that He would see of the travail of His soul, and be satisfied, for He would see a multitude of the human race saved, eternally saved.

Behold our Saviour in Gethsemane beneath the crushing weight of the sins of the whole world—betrayed into the hands of the murderous mob. It was a night of horror. He was forsaken by His best loved disciples— mocked, insulted, tortured, and finally condemned to die. Behold the Patient Sufferer.

As He passes the gate of Pilate's court, the cross which had been prepared for Barabbas was laid upon His bruised and bleeding shoulders....The Saviour's burden was too heavy for Him in His weak and suffering condition.... human nature could bear no more. He fell fainting beneath the burden." *Desire of Ages*, pp. 685-694, 741, 742.

"Our Saviour purchased the human race by humiliation of the very severest kind." *In Heavenly Places*, p. 53.

Another was chosen to carry the cross. On He trudged and willingly surrendered Himself to be hung naked on a cruel cross, shamed and humiliated.

Each blow of the hammer and the excruciating pain all for you and me. What love, agape love—self-sacrificing love—willing to say good-bye to life forever and die the second death that man might live.

"The Saviour could not see through the portals of the tomb. Hope did not present to Him His coming forth from the grave a conqueror, or tell Him of the Father's acceptance of the sacrifice. He feared that sin was so offensive to God that their separation was to be eternal. Christ felt the anguish which the sinner will feel when mercy shall no longer plead for the guilty race. It was the sense of sin, bringing the Father's wrath upon Him as man's substitute, that made the cup He drank so bitter, and broke the heart of the Son of God....So great was this agony that His physical pain was hardly felt." *Desire of Ages*, p. 753.

"Yet amid it all His love grew stronger and stronger." 2 Testimonies, p. 212. He was giving to you and me the hope of eternal life. Those nails that crucified Jesus were my sins, they killed Him and broke His heart. Truly, we have been loved with "an everlasting love", with such tenderness and yet so little gratitude and so much rebellion on our part. This is a message of love from Jesus, our Saviour, with nail print scars, still trying to rescue and save us. "For God so loved the world, He gave His only begotten Son, that whosoever believeth in Him should not perish, but have everlasting life." John 3:16.

If you wish to know more of God's love and our Best Friend, Jesus, write to:

Caring Kitchens,
Box 123,
Grimsby, Ontario
L3M 4G3

and ask for the free *Bible Studies*.

May God bless you with His love
and
remember God loves you.

Recipe Index

ENTRÉES